I0504143

France

Cultural Awareness and Business Negotiations

Country Study

Contents

INTRODUCTION

In our increasingly interconnected world, understanding and embracing cultural diversity has become essential for both personal and professional success. This series of Cultural Awareness books aims to provide participants with the knowledge, skills, and tools necessary to better understand and navigate various cultural contexts. By investing in cultural awareness, we are not only fostering stronger relationships but also paving the way for more successful business ventures and personal growth.

The expanding Global market presents immense opportunities for businesses. However, these opportunities come with the responsibility of understanding the nuances of various cultures. Unintentional cultural misunderstandings can jeopardise your chances of securing a crucial foothold in this lucrative market. This series highlights the importance of being aware of cultural differences and equips you with the tools to deal with the challenges that may arise when interacting with individuals from different cultural backgrounds.

Individuals and families who have travelled or are planning to move to different countries also face the challenge of adapting to new cultures. Culture shock can be overwhelming if one is not prepared to handle the changes that come with relocating. This course offers practical insights and tools to help individuals and families better understand and navigate the complexities of their new cultural environment.

Cultural awareness goes beyond learning facts or memorizing customs; it is about cultivating a genuine appreciation for the richness of human experiences. This series encourages participants to look beyond their own cultural lens and develop empathy for the perspectives of others. By doing so, we foster a more inclusive and harmonious world where people from diverse backgrounds can come together and create meaningful connections.

Throughout this book, you will be introduced to various cultural frameworks, practices, and traditions, as well as common misconceptions and stereotypes that often contribute to misunderstandings and miscommunications. Engaging with these topics will enable you to recognise cultural differences, appreciate their value, and navigate them effectively.

In conclusion, cultural awareness is essential for anyone aiming to expand their reach in the global market, adapt to new cultural environments, or enrich their lives by embracing the beauty of human diversity. By undertaking this journey, you are taking a significant step toward creating a more inclusive, empathetic, and successful future.

Ask yourself: Can you afford to miss out on the vital opportunities and personal growth that cultural awareness can bring to your life? The time to invest in cultural understanding is now. Welcome to an enlightening and transformative journey.

WallaceLine.com.au

By fusing cultural understanding with business acumen, we empower families, travellers and organisations to navigate global landscapes seamlessly. We're your intercultural guides, igniting opportunities, fostering negotiations, and bridging divides. Together, we unlock the power of diversity in the world.

How this book is structured?

This book is designed to serve as a guide, offering insights and advice on various countries. It is not intended to be read in one go, but rather as a set of snapshots and references providing valuable insights on a particular countries' lifestyles. As you explore the chapters, you may notice some overlap between topics, as certain strategies are applicable across different aspects of life in that country. Please read at your own pace, revisit sections as needed.

If you have any ideas on new input, or even corrections, we are more than happy to hear from you, and if our editors like and accept the input, then – if you are comfortable with it – we will include in our next update, with credit noted for you

Email us – contact@wallaceline.com.au

1. WHAT IS CULTURE?

What is Culture?

The Culture of a people can be understood as the system of shared ideas and meanings, explicit and implicit, which a people use to interpret the world, and which serve to pattern their behaviour.

This includes an understanding of the art, literature, and history of a society, but also less tangible aspects such as attitudes, prejudices, folklore etc. Unconscious or conscious habits are just as important as art and history.

Values - What people say one ought to do or not do? What is considered good or bad - the importance of honesty, or chastity?

Laws - What political authorities have decided people should do, and what the sanctions are?

Rules - What a society has decided its members should do. Social rules about marriage ages, childrearing.

Social Categories- Ways of thinking about people as types. - "friends", "criminals", "lovers", "nobles", "clergy".

Tacit Models - Implicit standards and patterns of behaviour that a person does not think about - knowing how to address a police officer rather than friends. Knowing how to dress for a job interview as opposed to a dance.

Fundamental - Categories and ways of thinking that people take for granted and may not recognise even when pointed out. - thinking in dualities good/bad, male/female.

Culture shapes

- The way we think
- The way we interact
- The way we communicate
- The way we transmit knowledge to the next generation

Culture manifests itself in

- Food
- Religion
- Dress
- Differences in language
- Our expectations of male and female roles
- Non-verbal rules and body language

The first step is in understanding the values and rules for behaviour of our own culture - the "normal" or "right" way of doing things. What makes us different?

Geert Hofstede

Between 1967 and 1973 Geert Hofstede conducted a study on culture across 100 000 employees of IBM in 50 countries. From this he developed a framework to 'measure' the 'value dimensions' of various cultures.

Hofstede identified 4 values which can be related to each culture:

- Individualism
- Masculinity
- Power Distance, and
- Uncertainty Avoidance

Later studies by Trompenaar have added several more; however, I will address the 4 basic values along with one later addition relating to time.

From surveys, Hofstede was able to map the cultures and compare them, and from this extrapolate as to why a culture may act in a particular way.

Taking the basic values separately, measured on a scale of 0 to 100:

	PD	ID	M	UA	LT
FR	68H	71H	43L	86H	63H
AUS	38L	90H	61H	51M	21L
USA	40	91	62	46	26
UK	35	89	66	35	51

H = top third of countries

M = medium

L = bottom third

Power Distance

In this dimension, we explore the concept that not all individuals within societies are equal, reflecting the culture's attitude towards these disparities. Power Distance is defined as the degree to which less powerful members of institutions and organizations within a country anticipate and accept that power is distributed unevenly.

With a Power Distance score of **68**, France demonstrates a relatively high acceptance of power inequality. In this society, children are often raised to maintain a certain level of emotional dependency on their parents, which later transitions to teachers and eventually superiors in the workplace. As a result, some degree of inequality is considered normal. Power tends to be centralized not only within companies and the government but also geographically, as evidenced by the majority of highways in France leading to Paris.

Many comparative studies reveal that French companies typically possess one or two additional hierarchical levels compared to similar organizations in Germany and the UK. Superiors in France enjoy certain privileges and can be difficult to access. The CEOs of large companies are often referred to as "Mr. PDG" (President Director General), a title that carries greater prestige than CEO. These PDGs often hold degrees from the country's most elite institutions, known as "*grandes écoles*," or "big schools."

Individualism v. Collectivism

This dimension addresses the level of interdependence that a society maintains among its members, focusing on whether individuals perceive themselves in terms of "I" or "We." In individualistic societies, people are expected to take care of themselves and their immediate family members only. In collectivist societies, individuals belong to 'in-groups' (such as families, clans, or organizations) that provide care and support in exchange for loyalty.

France, with a score of **71**, is characterized as an individualistic society. Parents typically raise their children to be emotionally independent from the groups they belong to, fostering a mindset focused on taking care of oneself and one's family.

The unique combination of high Power Distance and high Individualism in France is found in only a few other countries, such as Belgium, and to some extent, Spain and northern Italy. This pairing seemingly creates a contradiction; however, it merely provides a structured reflection of reality.

In France, this combination manifests itself in various ways:

- The family unit in France maintains a stronger emotional bond compared to other individualistic cultures, likely due to the high Power Distance and increased respect for the elderly.

- Subordinates typically show formal respect and deference to their superiors but may behave differently behind their backs. This is a result of the high Power Distance and the belief that they know better, despite not being able to express their opinions openly.

- The French often resort to strikes, revolts, and revolutions to reject those in power, as they believe that change cannot occur through gradual evolution. Employers and trade unions rarely engage in productive discussions, viewing each other as almost belonging to separate species.

- The need to distinguish between work and private life is even more significant in France than in the US, despite the US having a higher Individualism score. This distinction results from the emotional dependence of French employees on their bosses' words and actions.

- French citizens prefer to rely on the central government, an impersonal power centre that cannot easily invade their private lives. This preference for strong leadership during crises is common in France, but once the crisis is resolved, the president should step back and allow for weaker leadership.

- Many French people aspire to become leaders, whether as a mayor of a small village or as the chairperson of a local club.

- Customer service in France may seem inadequate from the perspective of Anglo-Saxons who believe the customer is king. However, the French are driven by their motivation to excel in their trades and expect respect for their skills before they are willing to provide excellent service.

Overall, France's cultural landscape is shaped by its unique combination of high Power Distance and Individualism, which impacts various aspects of French society, from family life to workplace dynamics.

Masculinity v. Femininity

A high score (Masculine) on this dimension signifies that a society is driven by competition, achievement, and success, where success is defined by being the winner or the best in one's field. This value system starts in school and continues throughout organizational life.

A low score (Feminine) on this dimension indicates that the dominant values in society prioritize caring for others and quality of life. In a Feminine society, quality of life is considered a sign of success, and standing out from the crowd is not admired. The fundamental issue here is what motivates people: wanting to be the best (Masculine) or enjoying what they do (Feminine).

With a score of **43**, France exhibits a moderately Feminine culture. This is evident in aspects such as the country's renowned welfare system (sécurité sociale), the 35-hour workweek, the annual five-week vacation, and an emphasis on the quality of life. However, French culture presents a unique characteristic within the context of the model: the upper class leans Feminine, while the working class leans Masculine. This distinction has not been observed in any other country and manifests itself in various ways:

- Top managers in France generally earn less than one might expect given the country's high Power Distance score.
- Historically, high society married couples could openly maintain relationships with lovers without facing negative consequences, a concept foreign to many cultures, including the US, as evidenced by the Clinton-Lewinsky scandal.
- Crimes of passion, or "crime passionel," have traditionally been met with more lenient sentences compared to other murder cases in France.

In summary, France's moderately Feminine culture is characterized by its focus on welfare, work-life balance, and quality of life. The unique distinction between the upper and working classes further sets it apart from other countries in terms of cultural values.

Uncertainty Avoidance

The Uncertainty Avoidance dimension addresses how societies cope with the fact that the future is always uncertain: should we attempt to control the future or simply let it unfold? The inherent ambiguity in the future creates anxiety, and different cultures have developed various ways to manage this anxiety. The extent to which a culture's members feel threatened by ambiguous or unknown situations and have established beliefs and institutions to mitigate these uncertainties is reflected in their Uncertainty Avoidance score.

With a score of **86**, French culture exhibits a high level of Uncertainty Avoidance. This preference for predictability and structure is apparent in various aspects of French society:

- The French dislike surprises and prefer well-structured plans. They often request comprehensive information before meetings and negotiations. This penchant for organization contributes to France's success in developing complex technologies and systems within stable environments, such as nuclear power plants, high-speed trains, and the aviation industry.
- High Uncertainty Avoidance, combined with high Power Distance and Individualism, creates a need for emotional safety valves. As a result, the French are known for being talkative and frequently expressing their opinions candidly, even if it means giving someone a piece of their mind.
- French society emphasizes the importance of laws, rules, and regulations to provide structure. However, this doesn't necessarily mean that all citizens adhere to them. Power holders, due to their privileges stemming from high Power Distance, may not feel obliged to follow every rule designed for the general population. Similarly, commoners often seek connections with power holders to claim exceptions to certain rules.

In summary, French culture's high Uncertainty Avoidance manifests in a preference for structure, planning, and adherence to rules, although these rules may not be uniformly followed by all members of society.

Long Term Orientation

France has a high score of 63 in the Pragmatism dimension, indicating that its culture leans towards being pragmatic. In pragmatic societies, people believe that truth is often contingent on the situation, context, and time. Key characteristics of these societies include:

- Flexibility: Individuals in pragmatic cultures are able to adapt traditions to evolving conditions, ensuring that customs and practices remain relevant.
- Financial responsibility: Pragmatic societies tend to exhibit a strong inclination towards saving and investing, promoting financial stability and growth.
- Thriftiness: People in these cultures are usually careful with their resources and mindful of their spending habits.
- Perseverance: Pragmatic societies are characterized by determination and persistence in achieving desired results, demonstrating a steadfast approach to accomplishing their goals.

In conclusion, France's high score in the Pragmatism dimension reflects its adaptable, financially responsible, and goal-oriented culture.

Acculturation

Acculturation is the process of adapting to a new culture.

- Variables affecting Acculturation
- The amount of time spent in the process – educating yourself
- The quantity and quality of interaction – trying things
- Ethnicity or nation of origin – how far is it removed from our own
- Affinity – willingness to learn and adapt

Stages of Acculturation

- Acceptance of new culture - honeymoon
- Individual starts to feel comfortable in the new culture
- Feelings of anger, hostility, and frustration
- Recovery
- Culture Shock

Generalisations

We should remember that there will probably never be one person within a culture that actually meets these dimensions. Rather this is a tool to anticipate likely reaction of a particular culture. There is never an average person! What should be remembered is that between the extremes, patterns do exist.

The inverse also applies; do not confuse a particular individual's personality as representative of culture. Whilst Australian's are considered sports loving people, there are people who don't like Rugby – as hard as that is to believe!

Stereotyping – setting a standard idea, concept or form. This 'notion' has a deeper meaning to our basic survival instincts.

Bias – a particular tendency or preference, which may prevent unprejudiced consideration of a topic. A 'learned' response.

Prejudice - an unfavourable opinion formed beforehand or without knowledge or reason.

Linear and Circular Thinking

How does culture affect Management?

Our Western (Greek) method of teaching & learning is if there is a problem then I can solve it. We are taught to identify issues as a 'problem' that challenges us. The individual works out a plan and overcomes the problem.

In a culture not rooted in the Western traditions, the issue may not be seen as a 'problem'!! Rather it is a divergence or even a side issue that can be avoided or not confronted until a solution is evident

Managing Across Culture

The management theory of MBI (Mapping – Bridging – Integrating) was developed to understand the differences and work out optimum paths to achieve greater workflows.

2. INTRODUCTION

The Importance of Cultural Awareness for Families and Business

In today's increasingly interconnected world, understanding and embracing different cultures is essential for both personal and professional success. With the advent of globalization and the ease of international travel, families and businesses alike find themselves navigating new cultural landscapes. For those moving to or conducting business in another country, cultivating cultural awareness is crucial to ensure a smooth transition and build lasting relationships in this vibrant country.

For families relocating, cultural awareness is the key to integrating successfully into their new home. By understanding the customs, values, and social norms of a society, families can better adapt to their surroundings and foster meaningful connections with their new neighbours. Familiarizing oneself with the language, local etiquette, and traditions can help ease the challenges of adjusting to a new environment, allowing families to fully immerse themselves in the rich cultural tapestry of a new country.

In the realm of business, cultural awareness is equally important. As countries continue to grow as economic powers, many international companies and entrepreneurs are seizing opportunities in the dynamic markets. Mastering the intricacies of business culture can help professionals negotiate deals effectively, avoid misunderstandings, and forge strong partnerships with their counterparts. By respecting local customs and demonstrating cultural sensitivity, businesspeople can build trust and credibility, essential ingredients for success in any international venture.

This comprehensive guide aims to equip families and professionals with the knowledge and tools necessary to embrace a foreign culture and thrive in their personal and professional lives. Through an exploration of history, values, and social norms, readers will gain valuable insights into the intricacies of a society. Additionally, practical advice on navigating daily life, social interactions, and business negotiations will empower families and professionals alike to make the most of their time in this captivating country.

As you embark on your journey, remember that cultural awareness is an ongoing process, requiring patience, openness, and a willingness to learn. By embracing the unique qualities that make a different culture such a fascinating place to live and work, you can create lasting memories, foster meaningful relationships, and unlock the full potential of your experience in this remarkable country.

Why France is a great destination for expats

Rich cultural heritage

France is renowned for its rich history, art, and architecture, making it a fascinating destination for expats. The country boasts numerous UNESCO World Heritage sites, world-class museums, and historical landmarks that offer countless opportunities for exploration and cultural immersion.

High quality of life

France consistently ranks highly in global quality of life indices due to its excellent healthcare, education, and social security systems. Expats can enjoy a comfortable lifestyle with access to a wide range of amenities and services.

Gastronomy

French cuisine is considered one of the finest in the world, with a diverse range of regional specialties, fresh produce, and world-class wine. Expats can relish in the country's culinary delights, whether dining out or preparing meals at home with local ingredients.

Business opportunities

France has a strong economy and is a leading global player in industries such as aerospace, automotive, luxury goods, and renewable energy. The country offers numerous opportunities for business professionals and entrepreneurs looking to advance their careers or establish a new venture.

Education

France is home to some of the world's top universities and research institutions, making it an ideal destination for students and academics. The country's education system is well-regarded, and expats can benefit from a wide range of educational opportunities for themselves and their families.

Geographical location

France's central location in Europe makes it an ideal base for expats who want to explore the continent. With an extensive rail network and numerous international airports, it is easy to travel to other European destinations for both work and leisure.

Language

While French is the official language, English is widely spoken in major cities and tourist areas, making it easier for expats to navigate their new environment. Learning French can also be a rewarding experience, offering deeper insights into the local culture and fostering better connections with the French people.

Vibrant expat community

France is home to a diverse and thriving expat community, providing ample opportunities for networking, socializing, and support. There are numerous clubs, organizations, and online resources catering specifically to the needs of expats, helping newcomers adapt to their new surroundings more easily.

Overall, France offers a unique and enriching experience for expats seeking to embrace a new culture, advance their careers, or simply enjoy a high quality of life. With its combination of history, culture, cuisine, and natural beauty, France is truly a destination worth discovering.

3. UNDERSTANDING FRENCH CULTURE

A Brief History

France has a rich and complex history that spans thousands of years. Here is a brief overview of some key events and periods in French history:

Prehistory

The prehistoric period in France is an essential chapter in the story of human evolution and cultural development. The region has a wealth of archaeological sites that provide insights into the lives of early humans, their art, and their interaction with the environment.

Evidence of early human habitation in France can be traced back to around 1.8 million years ago. The discovery of stone tools and fossil remains in various parts of the country has provided vital clues about the presence of early human species such as Homo erectus and Homo heidelbergensis. These early hominids were hunters and gatherers who relied on their physical strength and intelligence to survive in a challenging and ever-changing environment.

Over time, various human species evolved and adapted to the changing conditions in France. The most well-known of these species is the Neanderthal, who lived in the region between 400,000 and 40,000 years ago. Neanderthals were skilled hunters who used stone tools, such as hand axes and scrapers, to process animal carcasses and shape wooden tools. They were also known to use fire for cooking, warmth, and protection.

The arrival of Homo sapiens in France, around 45,000 years ago, marked a turning point in the region's prehistory. The Cro-Magnon people, as they were known, were anatomically similar to modern humans and brought with them new cultural practices and advanced technologies. They are credited with the creation of some of the earliest known artwork, including the remarkable cave paintings found at sites such as Lascaux and Chauvet.

The Lascaux cave paintings, created around 15,000 BCE, are among the most famous examples of prehistoric art in the world. Located in the Dordogne region of south-western France, the Lascaux caves contain a vast array of images depicting animals, humans, and abstract symbols. These paintings offer a glimpse into the lives, beliefs, and artistic sensibilities of the Palaeolithic people who inhabited the area.

The artists who created the Lascaux paintings used natural pigments, such as ochre and charcoal, to produce a range of colours and shades. They skilfully utilized the contours of the cave walls to add depth and perspective to their images. The artwork at Lascaux features a variety of animals, including horses, bison, aurochs, and deer, many of which were important sources of food and clothing for the people who lived in the region.

In addition to the Lascaux cave paintings, France is home to numerous other prehistoric sites that offer insights into the lives and culture of early humans. The Chauvet Cave, discovered in 1994, contains some of the oldest known cave paintings, dating back around 32,000 years. The artwork at Chauvet is remarkably well-preserved, thanks to a rockslide that sealed the entrance to the cave thousands of years ago.

Other important prehistoric sites in France include the rock shelters of La Madeleine and Laugerie-Basse, which provide evidence of the daily lives of Paleolithic people, including their tools, weapons, and food remains. Megalithic structures such as the Carnac stones and the menhirs of Brittany offer further glimpses into the prehistoric past, showcasing the ingenuity and creativity of the people who lived in France thousands of years ago.

In conclusion, the prehistoric period in France is marked by the presence of early human species, the development of advanced tools and technologies, and the creation of some of the world's oldest and most impressive artwork. The Lascaux cave paintings and other archaeological sites throughout the country offer a fascinating glimpse into the lives of the people who inhabited the region during this distant era, helping us to better understand the origins of human culture and the development of our species.

Celtic Gaul

The period of Celtic Gaul, which began around the 5th century BCE, marked a significant chapter in the history of France. The Gauls, a group of Celtic tribes, migrated to the region from central Europe and established a complex society characterized by trade, settlements, and cultural exchange.

The Gauls were a diverse and widespread group of tribes that shared a common Celtic language, known as Gaulish, and many cultural traditions. They lived in small, fortified settlements called oppida, which were typically located on high ground to provide natural defence. These settlements were the centers of political, economic, and social life for the Gauls, as well as hubs for artisans and craftsmen who produced goods like pottery, textiles, and metalwork.

One of the defining features of Gaulish society was its hierarchical structure, which was based on a combination of tribal and kinship ties. At the top of this hierarchy were the warrior aristocracy, who were responsible for maintaining order and organizing military campaigns. Below them were the freemen, who made up the bulk of the population and engaged in farming, crafts, and trade. At the bottom of the social ladder were slaves, who were captured in battle or born into servitude.

The Gauls were skilled farmers and herders, and their agricultural practices transformed the landscape of modern-day France. They cultivated a variety of crops, including wheat, barley, and rye, and raised animals such as cattle, sheep, and pigs. This agricultural wealth allowed the Gauls to establish a network of trade routes that connected their settlements to neighbouring regions, facilitating the exchange of goods, ideas, and technologies.

Trade was a vital aspect of Gaulish society and played a significant role in its development. The Gauls traded with neighbouring tribes and more distant peoples, such as the Etruscans in Italy and the Greeks in the Mediterranean. This trade brought a wealth of goods and ideas to the region, including luxury items like wine and pottery, as well as advanced technologies and artistic styles. The Gauls were particularly known for their skill in metalworking, producing exquisite gold, silver, and bronze artifacts that showcased their craftsmanship and artistic talent.

Religion was an important aspect of Gaulish culture, and the tribes worshipped a diverse pantheon of gods and goddesses. Many of these deities were associated with natural elements, such as the earth, water, and sky, reflecting the close relationship between the Gauls and their environment. Religious rituals and ceremonies were overseen by a class of priests called druids, who were also responsible for maintaining the oral traditions and legal system of the tribes.

The Gauls were a formidable military force and frequently engaged in conflicts with their neighbours. They were known for their fierce fighting style and the use of advanced weapons, such as the longsword and the war chariot. However, their decentralized political structure made it difficult for them to unite against a common enemy, which would ultimately prove to be their downfall.

In the 1st century BCE, the Roman Empire, under the leadership of Julius Caesar, began its conquest of Gaul. Despite initial resistance from the Gallic tribes, the Romans eventually subdued the region and incorporated it into their empire. The Roman conquest brought significant changes to Gaul, including the introduction of new technologies, urbanization, and the Latin language. However, the Gauls left an indelible mark on the cultural landscape of modern-day France, and their legacy can still be seen in the country's language, art, and traditions.

Roman Gaul

The conquest of Gaul by Julius Caesar in the 1st century BCE marked a transformative moment in the history of the region that would become modern-day France. Roman rule brought about significant changes in the political, economic, and cultural landscape of Gaul, transforming it into a prosperous and thriving province of the Roman Empire.

The conquest of Gaul began in 58 BCE, when Julius Caesar, then a Roman general, launched a military campaign to subdue the various Gallic tribes. The ensuing Gallic Wars lasted for almost a decade, with Caesar's forces facing fierce resistance from the Gauls, led by charismatic leaders such as Vercingetorix. Despite their initial successes, the Gauls were ultimately defeated in 51 BCE at the Battle of Alesia, effectively bringing the region under Roman control.

Under Roman rule, Gaul was reorganized into several provinces, the most important of which was Gallia Narbonensis in the south, Gallia Lugdunensis in the central-eastern region, and Gallia Belgica in the north. The Roman administration introduced new systems of governance, taxation, and infrastructure, which helped to promote economic growth and foster greater political stability.

One of the most significant developments during the Roman period was the growth of urban centers throughout Gaul. Roman cities, such as Lugdunum (modern-day Lyon), Narbonne, and Trier, became important hubs of trade, culture, and administration. These cities were characterized by their impressive architecture, including grand temples, amphitheatres, and aqueducts, which showcased the technological prowess and artistic sophistication of the Roman Empire.

Lugdunum, in particular, grew into a thriving metropolis under Roman rule. Founded in 43 BCE by the Roman general Lucius Munatius Plancus, Lugdunum was strategically located at the confluence of the Rhône and Saône rivers, making it an ideal centre for trade and transportation. The city became the capital of the province of Gallia Lugdunensis and the seat of the governor, giving it significant political and administrative importance.

The prosperity of Roman Gaul was built on its rich natural resources and agricultural wealth. The region was renowned for its fertile land, which supported the cultivation of a wide variety of crops, including wheat, olives, and grapes. Wine production, in particular, became a major industry in Gaul, with vineyards spreading throughout the region and Gallic wines gaining a reputation for their quality and flavour. The export of these products to other parts of the Roman Empire further fuelled the growth of the Gallic economy.

In addition to its economic achievements, Roman Gaul also experienced a flourishing of art and culture. The fusion of Gallic and Roman traditions gave rise to a unique cultural identity, which was reflected in the region's art, literature, and religious practices. Roman Gaul was home to numerous talented craftsmen and artists, who created stunning mosaics, frescoes, and sculptures that adorned public buildings and private homes alike.

The Romanization of Gaul had a profound and lasting impact on the region's identity, as many aspects of Gallic culture were assimilated into the broader Roman way of life. The Latin language, for example, gradually replaced the native Gaulish tongue, and many Gauls adopted Roman names and customs. However, this process of assimilation was not without resistance, as some elements of Gaulish culture and identity persisted throughout the Roman period and beyond.

The Franks

In the 5th century CE, as the Western Roman Empire began to crumble under the pressure of internal strife and external invasions, Germanic tribes such as the Franks took advantage of the weakening empire and began to migrate into Roman Gaul. Under the leadership of Clovis I, the Franks not only united the region but also established the Merovingian dynasty, which laid the foundation for the future kingdom of France. Clovis' conversion to Christianity played a crucial role in the spread of the religion throughout his kingdom, fostering a cultural transformation that would shape the region for centuries to come.

The Franks were a confederation of Germanic tribes that originated in the Lower and Middle Rhine region. In the late 4th and early 5th centuries CE, they began to expand their territory, moving into Roman Gaul and establishing themselves as a formidable power in the region. The fragmentation of the Roman Empire, coupled with the arrival of other barbarian tribes such as the Visigoths, Vandals, and Huns, created an environment of instability and conflict in which the Franks were able to thrive.

Clovis I, who came to power around 481 CE, emerged as a prominent leader of the Franks and embarked on a series of military campaigns to consolidate his rule over the various Frankish tribes and neighbouring regions. His victories over rival Germanic tribes, such as the Alemanni and the Visigoths, as well as the remnants of the Roman administration in Gaul, enabled him to establish a unified Frankish kingdom that encompassed much of modern-day France, Belgium, and western Germany.

One of the most significant events during Clovis' reign was his conversion to Christianity. In 496 CE, following a decisive victory over the Alemanni, Clovis converted to the Nicene form of Christianity, the faith of the Roman Empire, and was baptized by Saint Remigius, the bishop of Reims. His conversion marked a turning point in the history of the Frankish kingdom and had profound implications for the spread of Christianity throughout the region.

Clovis' adoption of Christianity provided him with a powerful tool for political and cultural unification. The religion offered a common framework of beliefs and values that could help to bind together the diverse peoples within his kingdom, many of whom were of Roman, Gallo-Roman, or Germanic descent. Furthermore, Clovis' alliance with the Roman Catholic Church granted him legitimacy in the eyes of both his subjects and neighbouring rulers, as well as access to valuable resources and networks of influence.

Following his conversion, Clovis actively promoted the spread of Christianity throughout his kingdom. He supported the construction of churches and monasteries and encouraged the growth of a native clergy that could minister to the spiritual needs of his people. The Christian faith became deeply intertwined with the political and social fabric of the Frankish kingdom, shaping its laws, customs, and institutions.

Under the Merovingian dynasty, which Clovis founded, the Frankish kingdom continued to expand and evolve. The dynasty was characterized by a complex system of governance, in which power was often divided among multiple kings and nobles. Although the Merovingians faced numerous challenges, including internal rivalries and external threats, their rule laid the groundwork for the Carolingian dynasty, which would eventually give rise to the Holy Roman Empire and the Kingdom of France.

Carolingian Dynasty

The Carolingian dynasty emerged in the 8th century, replacing the Merovingians as the ruling power in the Frankish kingdom. With Pepin the Short as its first king, the Carolingians ushered in a new era of political and cultural progress. Pepin's son, Charlemagne, expanded the kingdom considerably and was crowned the first Holy Roman Emperor in 800 CE, marking a significant milestone in European history.

The rise of the Carolingian dynasty can be traced back to Charles Martel, the grandfather of Charlemagne, who served as the mayor of the palace under the Merovingian kings. His successful defence of Gaul against the Muslim invasion at the Battle of Tours in 732 CE not only halted the expansion of the Umayyad Caliphate but also bolstered the prestige of the Carolingian family. His son, Pepin the Short, leveraged this newfound influence to depose the last Merovingian king, Childeric III, and was crowned king of the Franks in 751 CE with the support of Pope Zachary.

During his reign, Pepin the Short consolidated power and sought to strengthen the kingdom's political and military foundations. He formed alliances with the papacy, which granted him additional legitimacy and paved the way for closer cooperation between the Frankish kingdom and the Catholic Church. Under Pepin's rule, the Frankish kingdom expanded its territory, incorporating Aquitaine in the southwest and Lombard-controlled areas in northern Italy.

Charlemagne, the son of Pepin the Short, ascended to the throne in 768 CE and embarked on a series of military campaigns that dramatically expanded the Frankish kingdom. He conquered the Lombards in Italy, subdued the Saxons in modern-day Germany, and established control over territories in present-day Austria, Hungary, and Spain. At its height, Charlemagne's empire encompassed much of Western and Central Europe, creating a political and cultural unity that had not been seen since the fall of the Western Roman Empire.

Charlemagne's reign is often referred to as the Carolingian Renaissance, a period marked by a revival of learning, arts, and culture. He sought to promote education and literacy throughout his realm, encouraging the establishment of schools and supporting the work of scholars, such as the Anglo-Saxon monk Alcuin of York. The Carolingian Renaissance laid the foundation for the development of medieval European culture and helped to preserve the intellectual heritage of the ancient world.

In 800 CE, Pope Leo III crowned Charlemagne as the Holy Roman Emperor, a title that acknowledged his authority over the vast territories he had conquered and his role as the protector of Christendom. The crowning of Charlemagne marked the beginning of the Holy Roman Empire, a political entity that would endure for more than a millennium and shape the course of European history.

The Carolingian dynasty continued to rule the Frankish kingdom after Charlemagne's death in 814 CE, but internal divisions and external pressures gradually weakened its authority. The Treaty of Verdun in 843 CE divided the empire among Charlemagne's grandsons, leading to the emergence of distinct political entities that would later become France, Germany, and Italy.

In conclusion, the Carolingian dynasty played a pivotal role in the development of medieval Europe. Under the leadership of Pepin, the Short and Charlemagne, the Frankish kingdom expanded its territories and influence, fostering a cultural renaissance that would shape the region for centuries to come. Charlemagne's crowning as the Holy Roman Emperor in 800 CE marked the establishment of a political entity that would leave a lasting legacy on European history, even as the Carolingian dynasty itself eventually gave way to new political powers.

Middle Ages

The Capetian dynasty emerged in 987 CE, initiating a process of gradual unification and centralization of France under a single monarchy. The Middle Ages in France were characterized by significant events such as the Crusades, the Hundred Years' War with England, and the rise of Gothic architecture, which together shaped the nation's political, social, and cultural landscape.

The Capetian dynasty began with the election of Hugh Capet as King of France, following the death of the last Carolingian king, Louis V. Hugh Capet's ascension marked the end of the Carolingian era and the beginning of a new chapter in French history. Over the course of several centuries, the Capetians and their successors expanded and consolidated their territories, gradually bringing the various regions of France under a single, centralized authority.

During the Middle Ages, France was deeply involved in the Crusades, a series of religious wars waged between Christians and Muslims for control of the Holy Land. French knights and nobles played prominent roles in these military campaigns, which spanned from the late 11th century to the late 13th century. The Crusades brought both glory and infamy to France, as the nation's warriors fought valiantly in distant lands, but also committed atrocities in the name of their faith.

One of the most defining conflicts in French history was the Hundred Years' War (1337-1453), a prolonged struggle between the Kingdom of France and the Kingdom of England for control of the French throne. The war was marked by a series of battles, sieges, and political intrigues, as well as the emergence of iconic figures such as Joan of Arc, who inspired French forces to persevere in the face of seemingly insurmountable odds. The Hundred Years' War ultimately ended in French victory, solidifying the nation's territorial integrity and reinforcing the authority of the monarchy.

The Middle Ages also saw the rise of Gothic architecture in France, a style that combined elements of Romanesque and Islamic design to create soaring, light-filled structures that remain iconic to this day. Gothic architecture first appeared in the 12th century with the construction of the Abbey Church of Saint-Denis, which served as a model for later cathedrals, including Notre-Dame de Paris, Chartres, and Amiens. These magnificent buildings embodied the spiritual aspirations of the age, while also showcasing the technological and artistic prowess of French architects and craftsmen.

The period of the Capetian dynasty and the Middle Ages more broadly was marked by considerable social and cultural changes in France. The emergence of a centralized monarchy provided the impetus for the development of a distinctive French identity, as various regions and peoples were gradually united under a single banner. The Crusades and the Hundred Years' War shaped the nation's military and political trajectory, while the rise of Gothic architecture signalled a new era of artistic and architectural innovation.

Renaissance and Reformation

The French Renaissance in the 16th century marked a period of significant cultural, artistic, and scientific advancements in France. This golden age was inspired by the Italian Renaissance and characterized by a flourishing of the arts, the spread of humanism, and an intellectual awakening that transformed French society. Simultaneously, the Protestant Reformation challenged the Catholic Church's dominance and gave rise to religious conflicts between Catholics and Huguenots (French Protestants), which greatly impacted the political landscape of the time.

The French Renaissance was a time of profound artistic and cultural growth, as painters, sculptors, architects, and writers embraced new ideas and techniques. Key figures such as Leonardo da Vinci, who spent his final years in France, and native talents like François Clouet and Jean Clouet, contributed to the development of French Art. Architectural wonders, such as the Château de Chambord and the Château de Fontainebleau, showcased the innovative and opulent designs of the period. French literature also flourished during the Renaissance, with writers such as François Rabelais, Michel de Montaigne, and Pierre de Ronsard producing ground-breaking works that continue to be celebrated today. This cultural explosion was fuelled by the patronage of French royalty, particularly King Francis I, who actively supported the arts and sought to make France a centre of learning and creativity.

The scientific advancements of the French Renaissance were similarly transformative, with scholars and thinkers delving into various fields of knowledge. The invention of the printing press enabled the rapid dissemination of ideas, helping to foster intellectual curiosity and debate. Notable French scholars, such as physician and botanist Jean Fernel, mathematician and philosopher Oronce Fine, and naturalist Pierre Belon, made significant contributions to their respective fields, further enhancing the reputation of France as a centre of learning and innovation.

While the French Renaissance saw an explosion of cultural, artistic, and scientific achievements, the 16th century was also a time of religious turmoil. The Protestant Reformation, initiated by Martin Luther in Germany, spread rapidly across Europe, including France. The rise of Protestantism challenged the authority of the Catholic Church, and many French people converted to the new faith, becoming known as Huguenots.

The growing influence of Protestantism in France led to a series of bloody conflicts known as the French Wars of Religion, which lasted from 1562 to 1598. These wars pitted Catholics against Huguenots, with both sides vying for control of the country and religious supremacy. The violence reached its peak during the infamous St. Bartholomew's Day Massacre in 1572, when thousands of Huguenots were murdered by Catholic mobs in Paris and other cities. The Wars of Religion culminated in the Edict of Nantes in 1598, issued by King Henry IV, a former Huguenot who had converted to Catholicism in order to claim the French throne. The Edict granted religious freedom and civil rights to Huguenots, bringing a measure of peace and stability to the country.

Absolute Monarchy

In the 17th and 18th centuries, France emerged as a powerful and influential nation under the absolute rule of monarchs such as Louis XIV. The era, often referred to as the Age of Absolutism, was characterized by the centralization of power, the expansion of French territory, and the rise of French culture and influence throughout Europe. During this period, France also experienced significant colonial expansion, particularly in North America and the Caribbean, which brought wealth and prestige to the nation.

Louis XIV, known as the Sun King, ruled France from 1643 to 1715 and is perhaps the most famous and powerful monarch of his time. He was determined to assert his absolute authority and strengthen the power of the monarchy, both domestically and internationally. One of his most notable achievements was the construction of the Palace of Versailles, which became a symbol of French grandeur and the centre of political power. Versailles showcased the opulence and extravagance of the French court, and it also served as a tool for controlling the nobility by requiring their presence at the palace.

Under Louis XIV, France embarked on a series of military campaigns to expand its borders and assert its dominance in Europe. The Sun King sought to make France the preeminent power on the continent, engaging in conflicts such as the War of Devolution, the Dutch War, and the War of the Spanish Succession. Although these wars were costly and not always successful, they did contribute to the expansion of French territory and the spread of French influence.

During the 17th and 18th centuries, France turned its attention to colonial expansion, driven by the desire for resources, trade, and prestige. French explorers and settlers ventured to North America, where they established colonies in present-day Canada and the Mississippi Valley, including New France (Quebec), Acadia, and Louisiana. France also established a foothold in the Caribbean, where colonies like Saint-Domingue (now Haiti), Martinique, and Guadeloupe became important centers of sugar and coffee production. The French colonial empire was driven by the mercantilist economic policy, which sought to enrich the mother country through the accumulation of wealth from its colonies.

The French colonial empire, however, was not without its challenges. Competition with other European powers, particularly England and Spain, led to numerous conflicts, including the Seven Years' War, which resulted in the loss of much of France's North American territory to Britain. Additionally, the harsh conditions in the colonies and the brutal treatment of enslaved people led to resistance and rebellion, including the Haitian Revolution, which ultimately resulted in the loss of France's most lucrative colony.

French Revolution

The French Revolution, which began in 1789, was a tumultuous period of radical social, political, and economic change in France. Discontent with the monarchy, rampant social inequality, and financial crises all contributed to the uprising, which ultimately abolished the monarchy and led to the execution of King Louis XVI and Queen Marie Antoinette. The revolution also paved the way for the rise of Napoleon Bonaparte, who became Emperor of the French in 1804.

At the heart of the French Revolution was a deep dissatisfaction with the existing political and social order, dominated by the Bourbon monarchy and a rigid, hierarchical class system. The nobility and clergy enjoyed significant privileges, while the majority of the population, known as the Third Estate, bore the brunt of taxation and struggled with poverty and economic hardship. The Enlightenment, a cultural and intellectual movement that emphasized reason and individualism, also played a significant role in shaping the revolutionary mindset, as it challenged traditional authority and advocated for democratic principles.

The French economy was also in dire straits, largely due to the country's involvement in a series of costly wars, including the American Revolution. In an attempt to address the financial crisis, King Louis XVI called for a meeting of the Estates-General in 1789, a legislative body consisting of representatives from the three estates: the clergy, the nobility, and the common people. However, tensions between the estates quickly escalated, and the Third Estate broke away to form the National Assembly, which aimed to create a new constitution that would limit the monarchy's power and promote greater social equality.

The revolution gained momentum in July 1789 with the storming of the Bastille, a prison in Paris that symbolized royal tyranny. This event marked the beginning of widespread violence and upheaval, as revolutionaries sought to dismantle the existing social and political structures. The monarchy was eventually abolished, and King Louis XVI and Queen Marie Antoinette were executed by guillotine in 1793, signalling the end of the Bourbon dynasty.

In the midst of the chaos and instability, a young military officer named Napoleon Bonaparte rose to prominence, demonstrating exceptional strategic and leadership skills. Napoleon's military successes in Italy and Egypt garnered him widespread admiration and support, and in 1799, he staged a coup that effectively ended the French Revolution and established him as the First Consul of France.

In 1804, Napoleon crowned himself Emperor of the French, ushering in a new era of French history known as the Napoleonic Era. As emperor, Napoleon implemented a series of sweeping reforms, including the establishment of the Napoleonic Code, a comprehensive legal system that remains the basis of French civil law to this day. Under Napoleon's rule, France expanded its territory and influence across much of Europe, but ultimately, his ambition and military aggression would lead to his downfall.

Napoleonic Era

Napoleon Bonaparte, who rose to power following the French Revolution, was a military genius and ambitious leader who expanded the French Empire and conquered much of Europe. Under his rule, France emerged as a dominant power on the European continent. However, Napoleon's relentless expansionism and military aggression eventually led to his downfall, culminating in his defeat in 1815 and the restoration of the Bourbon monarchy.

Napoleon's military conquests began soon after he assumed power. In 1800, he led the French army to victory against the Austrians in the Battle of Marengo, securing France's control over Italy. Over the next decade, Napoleon led his armies to numerous victories across Europe, toppling established monarchies and redrawing the political map of the continent. Among his notable conquests were the Austrian, Prussian, and Russian empires, as well as the Kingdom of Spain.

Napoleon's empire-building was driven by a desire to spread the ideals of the French Revolution and to consolidate his power. He implemented a series of far-reaching reforms in the territories under his control, including the introduction of the Napoleonic Code, which served as a model for modern civil law systems. Additionally, he established new legal and administrative structures, as well as promoted education, science, and the arts.

However, Napoleon's military success and expansionist ambitions were not without consequences. His aggressive policies antagonized the other European powers, leading to a series of costly and bloody wars known as the Napoleonic Wars. These conflicts took a heavy toll on the French army and the country's resources, ultimately undermining the stability of the empire.

Napoleon's empire began to unravel in 1812 when he invaded Russia. The disastrous campaign resulted in the loss of more than half a million soldiers and weakened the French military. This setback, combined with growing resistance from other European powers, led to a series of defeats for Napoleon and the eventual collapse of his empire.

In 1814, a coalition of European powers, led by Britain, Prussia, Austria, and Russia, defeated Napoleon's forces and forced him to abdicate the throne. He was exiled to the island of Elba, but his absence was short-lived. In 1815, Napoleon escaped from exile and returned to France, rallying his supporters and reclaiming power in a period known as the Hundred Days. However, his comeback was short-lived, as he was defeated by a coalition of European armies at the Battle of Waterloo in June 1815.

Following Napoleon's defeat at Waterloo, the Bourbon monarchy was restored in France, with King Louis XVIII ascending to the throne. The Congress of Vienna, a gathering of European powers, sought to establish a new balance of power on the continent and prevent the rise of another Napoleon-like figure. As a result, France's borders were redrawn, and the country was forced to relinquish many of its territorial gains.

19th Century

Throughout the 19th century, France experienced a series of political upheavals that reflected the nation's struggle to establish a stable government and find its footing in the rapidly changing European landscape. This period was marked by several revolutions and regime changes, including the 1830 July Revolution, the 1848 February Revolution, and the establishment of the Second Empire under Napoleon III. The culmination of these events was the Franco-Prussian War in 1870-71, which led to the fall of the Second Empire and the establishment of the Third Republic.

The 1830 July Revolution was sparked by growing dissatisfaction with the Bourbon monarchy, specifically the rule of King Charles X. His conservative policies, attempts to stifle freedom of the press, and efforts to restore the privileges of the nobility and the Catholic Church alienated many in French society. The revolution began with a series of street protests in Paris that forced Charles X to abdicate, leading to the installation of Louis-Philippe, the Duke of Orleans, as king. Louis-Philippe's reign, known as the July Monarchy, sought to bridge the gap between the conservative aristocracy and the liberal bourgeoisie. However, his regime was plagued by political unrest and economic hardship, which contributed to its eventual downfall.

In 1848, another revolution swept through France, fuelled by economic crisis, social inequality, and calls for democratic reform. The February Revolution led to the fall of the July Monarchy and the establishment of the Second French Republic. This new government instituted several progressive measures, including the abolition of slavery, universal male suffrage, and the right to work. However, internal divisions, financial difficulties, and the rise of radical socialist movements like the Paris Commune contributed to the instability of the Second Republic.

Amid the chaos, Louis-Napoleon Bonaparte, the nephew of Napoleon I, emerged as a popular figure who promised to restore order and stability. In 1851, he staged a coup d'état and declared himself Emperor Napoleon III, marking the beginning of the Second Empire. Napoleon III's rule was characterized by economic modernization, the expansion of the French Empire, and a focus on infrastructure development. Despite these successes, his regime was plagued by political repression and growing opposition from both conservatives and liberals.

The Second Empire's downfall was precipitated by the disastrous Franco-Prussian War in 1870-71. The war was sparked by tensions between France and the rising power of Prussia, which sought to unify the German states under its leadership. The French army, ill-prepared and poorly led, suffered a series of humiliating defeats, culminating in the capture of Napoleon III at the Battle of Sedan. The war had a profound impact on France, leading to the fall of the Second Empire and the establishment of the Third Republic.

The Third Republic, which lasted from 1871 to 1940, was characterized by a series of political crises and a deeply divided society. Despite these challenges, it proved to be the longest-lasting regime in French history up to that point. The Third Republic saw the rise of a new generation of political leaders, the expansion of public education, and the flourishing of the arts and sciences. However, it also faced numerous challenges, including the legacy of the Franco-Prussian War, the rise of radical political movements, and the ever-present threat of conflict in Europe.

20th Century

France played a crucial role in both World War I and World War II, serving as a major battleground and key participant in the conflicts. The repercussions of these wars left lasting impacts on the nation, shaping its political landscape and contributing to the establishment of successive republics.

During World War I, France was one of the Allied Powers, fighting alongside the United Kingdom, Russia, and later the United States, against the Central Powers led by Germany, Austria-Hungary, and the Ottoman Empire. The war was characterized by brutal trench warfare, particularly on the Western Front, which stretched across northern France. French troops suffered heavy casualties, with over 1.3 million lives lost and millions more wounded. Despite the immense human and material cost, the Allies emerged victorious, with the Treaty of Versailles in 1919 bringing an end to the conflict.

In the interwar years, France struggled to recover from the devastation of World War I. The country was burdened with enormous war debts, a weakened economy, and political instability that plagued the Third Republic. As global tensions mounted in the 1930s, France sought to strengthen its defences against potential aggression, most notably by constructing the Maginot Line along its border with Germany.

World War II saw France once again in the crosshairs of conflict. The country was invaded by Nazi Germany in 1940 and, after a rapid and disastrous military defeat, signed an armistice with the Axis powers. France was divided into an occupied zone in the north, controlled directly by the Nazis, and a nominally independent but collaborationist regime in the south, known as Vichy France. The French population endured the harsh realities of occupation, including food shortages, forced labour, and persecution of Jews and other minority groups.

Despite the occupation, a strong French Resistance movement emerged, conducting acts of sabotage, espionage, and providing aid to the Allied forces. The tide of the war began to turn in favour of the Allies with the 1944 D-Day landings in Normandy, which marked the beginning of the liberation of France. Paris was liberated in August 1944, and by the end of the year, most of the country was free from Nazi control.

In the aftermath of World War II, the Fourth Republic was established, aiming to address the shortcomings of the previous regime. While the new government oversaw economic recovery and the beginnings of decolonization, it faced ongoing political instability and was ultimately unable to manage the crisis sparked by the Algerian War of Independence.

The current Fifth Republic was established in 1958, with Charles de Gaulle as its first president. The new constitution strengthened the executive branch and provided a more stable framework for governance. Under de Gaulle's leadership, France withdrew from Algeria, pursued an independent foreign policy, and experienced a period of economic growth known as the "Trente Glorieuses" (Thirty Glorious Years). In the decades since its establishment, the Fifth Republic has weathered numerous challenges, including social unrest, economic crises, and global conflicts, while continuing to play a prominent role on the world stage.

Modern France

Today, France stands as a leading global power, boasting a strong economy, advanced infrastructure, and significant cultural and political influence. As a founding member of the European Union and the United Nations, France plays an essential role in shaping international policy and fostering cooperation among nations.

With the world's sixth-largest economy, France is an economic powerhouse. The country's diversified economy is built on a mix of sectors, including manufacturing, services, agriculture, and technology. France is renowned for its luxury goods, fashion, and gastronomy industries, as well as being a global leader in the aerospace, automotive, pharmaceutical, and nuclear power sectors. The French economy benefits from a well-educated and skilled workforce, thanks to a robust and accessible education system.

France's advanced infrastructure, including an extensive network of high-speed trains (TGV), highways, and seaports, facilitates domestic and international trade and contributes to the country's economic competitiveness. Furthermore, France's status as a prominent tourist destination, with iconic landmarks like the Eiffel Tower, Louvre Museum, and Palace of Versailles, generates significant revenue and fosters cultural exchange.

Culturally, France has a rich and storied history, as well as a contemporary scene that continues to thrive. French literature, philosophy, art, and cinema have made lasting impacts on the global stage, and the country is home to a large number of UNESCO World Heritage sites. France is also renowned for its contributions to gastronomy, with its cuisine and wine revered worldwide.

Politically, France is a stable democracy, governed by the principles of the Fifth Republic. The country's political system is characterized by a strong executive branch, with power shared between the president and the prime minister. France's parliament comprises two houses, the National Assembly and the Senate, which work together to create and enact legislation.

As a permanent member of the United Nations Security Council, France is a key player in international diplomacy and security. The country's armed forces are among the world's most capable and well-equipped, with significant expeditionary capabilities and a nuclear deterrent. France has been at the forefront of global efforts to combat terrorism, address climate change, and promote human rights, in addition to playing an active role in peacekeeping missions and humanitarian efforts.

As a member of the European Union, France has been instrumental in shaping the organization's policies and direction. The country is part of the Schengen Area, which allows for passport-free travel among its member states, and the Eurozone, which shares a common currency. Through its EU membership, France has fostered economic cooperation, political stability, and cultural exchange across the continent.

In conclusion, France is a leading global power with a strong economy, advanced infrastructure, and significant cultural and political influence. The country has played a crucial role in shaping international relations and promoting peace and cooperation among nations. As a founding member of both the European Union and the United Nations, France is well-positioned to continue exerting a positive impact on the world in the years to come.

Religion, Values, and Social Norms

Religion, values, and social norms play an important role in French society, shaping its culture, traditions, and way of life. As a predominantly secular nation, France upholds the principle of laïcité, or the separation of church and state, which ensures that religious beliefs remain a private matter and do not interfere with public affairs.

Religion

Historically, France has been predominantly Roman Catholic, and the **Catholic Church** has played a significant role in the country's history and culture. However, the influence of the Church has declined in recent decades, and a growing percentage of the population identifies as atheist or agnostic. According to recent surveys, around 41% of French people identify as Catholic, while 39% consider themselves to be non-religious. Other religious affiliations in France include Islam, Protestantism, and Judaism, which contribute to the country's religious diversity.

Values

French society is characterized by a strong emphasis on individualism, which is evident in the country's high score on the Individualism dimension of Hofstede's cultural model. This focus on individual rights and personal freedom is deeply ingrained in French culture and is reflected in the national motto "Liberté, Égalité, Fraternité" (Liberty, Equality, Brotherhood). Other core values in France include secularism, respect for privacy, and the importance of culture and the arts.

Social Norms

French social norms are shaped by the country's history, traditions, and values. Some key aspects of French social norms include:

Politeness and formality

French people often place great importance on politeness, courtesy, and proper etiquette. It is customary to greet others with a handshake or a kiss on the cheek, depending on the relationship, and to use formal titles such as "Monsieur" (Sir) or "Madame" (Madam) when addressing someone you don't know well.

The importance of language

The French language is a significant source of national pride, and fluency in French is highly valued. While many French people speak English, making an effort to learn and use French is appreciated and helps facilitate social interactions.

Respect for privacy

In line with their individualistic values, French people often maintain a clear distinction between their public and private lives, and respect for one's privacy is highly regarded.

Appreciation for food and gastronomy

French cuisine is celebrated worldwide, and the French are known for their appreciation of high-quality, fresh ingredients and their love for long, leisurely meals. Sharing a meal with family or friends is an important social ritual.

Work-life balance

France is known for its focus on work-life balance, with policies such as the 35-hour workweek and generous vacation time. The French value their leisure time and prioritize spending it with family and friends.

Language: Key Phrases and Expressions

Knowing some key phrases and expressions in French can greatly enhance your experience in France and help you communicate with locals. Here are some essential French phrases and expressions to get you started:

- Bonjour (bohn-zhoor) - Hello
- Au revoir (ohr-vwahr) - Goodbye
- Merci (mehr-see) - Thank you
- S'il vous plaît (seel-voo-play) - Please
- Excusez-moi (ex-kew-zay-mwah) - Excuse me
- Oui (wee) - Yes
- Non (nohn) - No
- Comment ça va? (koh-mahn sah vah) - How are you?
- Ça va bien (sah vah byan) - I'm fine
- Comment vous appelez-vous? (koh-mahn vooz-ah-play-voo) - What is your name?
- Je m'appelle... (zhuh mah-pehl) - My name is...
- Enchanté(e) (ahn-shahn-tay) - Nice to meet you
- Parlez-vous anglais? (par lay vooz-ahn-glay) - Do you speak English?
- Je ne parle pas français (zhuh nuh parl pah frahn-say) - I don't speak French
- Où sont les toilettes? (oo sohn lay twa-let) - Where are the restrooms?
- Combien ça coûte? (kohm-byahn sah koot) - How much does it cost?
- Pardon (pahr-dohn) - Sorry
- Je ne comprends pas (zhuh nuh kohm-prahn pah) - I don't understand
- Aidez-moi, s'il vous plaît (ay-day-mwah seel-voo-play) - Help me, please
- À tout à l'heure (ah toot ah leur) - See you later

Colloquial expressions

Colloquial expressions, or idiomatic phrases, are an important part of understanding everyday French conversation. Here are some common French colloquial expressions to help you better understand and engage with native speakers:

- Ça marche (sah marsh) - Okay, that works
- C'est la vie (say lah vee) - That's life, such is life
- Ça roule (sah rool) - Everything's going well
- On y va (ohn ee vah) - Let's go
- Laisse tomber (less tom-bay) - Let it go, never mind
- Ça te dit? (sah tuh dee) - Are you up for it?
- T'inquiète (tan-kee-yet) - Don't worry
- C'est pas grave (say pah grav) - It's not a big deal, no problem
- J'en ai marre (zhahn ay mar) - I'm fed up, I've had enough
- C'est n'importe quoi (say nehm-pohrt kwah) - That's nonsense, that's ridiculous
- Ça fait un bail (sah fay uhn bay) - It's been a while
- À plus tard (ah plew tar) - See you later
- À la prochaine (ah lah proh-shen) - Until next time
- T'es sérieux? (tay se-ree-yuh) - Are you serious? (informal)
- Pas de souci (pah duh soo-see) - No worries, no problem

By incorporating these colloquial expressions into your French conversations, you'll be able to better connect with native speakers and gain a deeper understanding of the language. Just remember that some expressions may be more informal than others, so be mindful of the context and the person you're speaking with.

Famous Myths and legends

France has a rich tradition of myths and legends that have been passed down through generations. Some of the most famous French myths and legends include:

- **King Arthur and the Knights of the Round Table**: Although King Arthur is often associated with British mythology, many of the stories surrounding his legend have strong connections to France, particularly the region of Brittany. The stories of the Knights of the Round Table, the search for the Holy Grail, and the love affair between Lancelot and Guinevere all have French origins.
- **The Beast of Gévaudan**: In the 18th century, a mysterious creature known as the Beast of Gévaudan terrorized the people of the former province of Gévaudan (now part of the Lozère and Haute-Loire departments). The beast was said to be a large, wolf-like creature that attacked and killed numerous people. The true nature of the beast has never been confirmed, and it remains a popular subject in French folklore.

- **Quasimodo and the Hunchback of Notre-Dame**: Victor Hugo's famous novel "The Hunchback of Notre-Dame" tells the story of Quasimodo, a deformed and isolated bell-ringer who falls in love with the beautiful gypsy Esmeralda. While not based on a specific historical figure or event, the novel has become an iconic part of French literature and has inspired numerous adaptations.
- **The Legend of Melusine**: Melusine is a mythical figure from French folklore, often depicted as a beautiful woman with the lower body of a serpent or a fish. She is said to have been a powerful fairy who married a mortal man, only to be betrayed by him when he discovered her secret. The legend of Melusine has inspired many French stories and works of art.
- **The Dames Blanches**: The Dames Blanches, or White Ladies, are spirits from French folklore, often depicted as beautiful women dressed in white. They are said to haunt various locations throughout France, particularly forests, rivers, and bridges. These spirits have been known to help or hinder travellers, depending on their behaviour.
- **The Song of Roland**: "The Song of Roland" is an epic poem from the 11th century that tells the story of Roland, a brave knight who served under the Frankish king Charlemagne. The poem describes the heroic deeds of Roland and his fellow knights as they defend their homeland against invading forces. The story is based on historical events but has been heavily embellished and romanticized over time.

4. ADAPTING TO DAILY LIFE

Housing and Accommodation

Adapting to daily life in France involves understanding the local housing market, knowing your rights as a tenant or homeowner, and ensuring you have the necessary utilities and services in place. With some research and preparation, you can find a suitable home and settle into life in France.

Types of housing

In France, you'll find a variety of housing options, including apartments (appartements), houses (maisons), and studios (studios). Apartments and studios are more common in urban areas, while houses are typically found in suburban or rural areas. Some people also choose to live in furnished residences (résidences meublées) or shared housing (colocations).

Finding a place to live

To search for housing in France, you can use online platforms such as **SeLoger**, **Leboncoin**, or **Bien'ici**. Local newspapers and real estate agencies (agences immobilières) are also useful resources. If you are moving to France for work, your employer may provide assistance with finding accommodation.

Renting

When renting a property in France, you'll typically need to sign a lease (bail) and provide a security deposit (dépôt de garantie). You may also be required to have a guarantor (garant) who will be financially responsible if you are unable to pay your rent. Be prepared to provide proof of income, identification, and rental history.

Rental costs

Rental costs in France can vary greatly depending on the location, size, and condition of the property. Generally, rent is more expensive in major cities like Paris, Lyon, and Marseille. Keep in mind that utilities (électricité, eau, gaz) and building charges (charges de copropriété) may not be included in the rent, so be sure to ask the landlord or agency about these additional costs.

Tenants' rights

France has strong tenant protection laws. As a tenant, you have the right to a habitable property and privacy. The landlord is responsible for making necessary repairs and maintaining the property. It is also illegal for a landlord to evict a tenant without proper cause and following a specific procedure.

Buying property

Purchasing property in France can be an attractive option for long-term residents. The process involves finding a property, making an offer, signing a preliminary contract (compromis de vente), obtaining a mortgage if necessary, and signing the final deed of sale (acte de vente) with a notary (notaire). It's essential to work with a notary, as they ensure the legality of the transaction and handle the transfer of ownership.

Home insurance

Whether you're renting or buying a property in France, it's important to have home insurance (assurance habitation) to protect against potential damages or losses. French law requires tenants to have a minimum level of insurance coverage, while homeowners are strongly advised to have comprehensive coverage.

Utilities and services

When moving into a new property, you'll need to set up your utilities (eau, électricité, gaz) and services such as internet, telephone, and television. You may need to open a new account with a utility provider or transfer an existing account from the previous occupant. It's essential to compare different providers to find the best rates and services for your needs.

Transportation and Getting Around

Navigating transportation options in France is relatively easy, thanks to the country's well-developed infrastructure and variety of travel options. Whether you're using public transportation, cycling, or driving, getting around France can be efficient and enjoyable.

Public transportation

France has an extensive and efficient public transportation network, particularly in major cities. Public transport options include buses, trams, and metro systems. Paris, Lyon, and Marseille have extensive metro networks, while many other cities have tram and bus systems. Public transportation is generally affordable, with single tickets, daily passes, or monthly subscriptions available.

Trains

The French national railway company, SNCF, operates a vast network of trains that connect cities and towns across the country. High-speed TGV trains link major cities, while regional trains (TER) serve smaller towns and rural areas. Train travel in France is comfortable and reliable, with tickets available for purchase online, at train stations, or through authorized agents.

Bicycles

Cycling is a popular mode of transportation in many French cities, with dedicated bike lanes and bike-sharing systems in place. Major cities like Paris, Lyon, and Bordeaux have public bike-sharing programs (**Vélib**, **Vélo'v**, and VCub, respectively), allowing you to rent a bike for a short period at a low cost.

Cars

While having a car can be convenient for exploring rural areas or traveling between cities, driving in France can be challenging due to traffic, limited parking, and toll roads. If you plan to drive in France, you will need a valid driver's license, insurance, and vehicle registration. International driving permits are accepted for short-term stays, but long-term residents may need to obtain a French driver's license.

Taxis and ride-sharing

Taxis are widely available in French cities and can be hailed on the street, booked in advance, or found at designated taxi ranks. Ride-sharing services like Uber and Bolt also operate in major cities. Keep in mind that taxis and ride-sharing services can be more expensive than public transportation.

Air travel

France has numerous airports, with Paris Charles de Gaulle and Orly being the largest. Domestic flights are available between major cities, but trains are often a faster and eco-friendlier alternative for shorter distances.

Long-distance buses

Intercity buses, operated by companies such as **FlixBus**, **BlaBlaBus**, and **Eurolines**, provide a budget-friendly option for traveling between cities and regions in France. While buses may take longer than trains, they often offer cheaper fares and serve a broader range of destinations.

Walking

Many French cities and towns are pedestrian-friendly, with well-maintained sidewalks, pedestrian zones, and historic centers that are best explored on foot. Walking is an excellent way to discover the local culture, architecture, and everyday life.

Education and Schooling Options

When considering schooling options in France, it's essential to consider factors such as language of instruction, curriculum, location, and cost. Expats may find it helpful to visit different schools and speak with other expat families to find the best fit for their children's needs and goals.

Public schools

France has a well-regarded public education system that is free for all residents, including expats. Public schools follow a national curriculum and are divided into three levels: primary schools (écoles primaires) for ages 6 to 11, middle schools (collèges) for ages 11 to 15, and high schools (lycées) for ages 15 to 18. Public schools are secular, and students are not permitted to wear religious symbols or attire. French is the primary language of instruction in public schools, which can be a challenge for non-French speaking students.

Private schools

Private schools in France can be either secular or religious, with Catholic schools being the most common. Private schools may follow the national curriculum or offer alternative programs, such as Montessori or Steiner-Waldorf education. Private schools charge tuition fees, which can vary depending on the school's reputation and location.

International schools

International schools cater to the needs of expat families and offer programs that follow the curricula of other countries, such as the British, American, or International Baccalaureate (IB) systems. These schools typically offer instruction in English or other languages and can be found in larger cities like Paris, Lyon, and Marseille. International schools charge tuition fees and may have limited spaces, so it's essential to apply early.

Bilingual schools

Bilingual schools in France offer education in both French and another language, such as English, Spanish, or German. These schools can be public or private and may follow the French national curriculum or an international program. Bilingual schools can be an excellent option for expat families who want their children to become fluent in French while maintaining their native language.

Home-schooling

Home-schooling is legal in France, but it is subject to strict regulations and oversight. Families must register with the local education authority and submit an annual inspection of their educational program. Home-schooling is relatively uncommon in France, and resources and support networks may be limited compared to other countries.

Higher education

France has a range of higher education institutions, including universities, grandes écoles, and specialized schools for art, business, and engineering. Higher education is typically taught in French, but some institutions offer English-taught programs. Tuition fees for public universities are relatively low compared to other countries, and financial aid is available for both French and international students.

Healthcare and Medical Facilities

Overall, France's healthcare system is known for its high standards and accessibility. Expats should familiarize themselves with the available healthcare options and ensure they have appropriate health insurance coverage to access the services they need.

Public healthcare

France has a high-quality public healthcare system, which is ranked among the best in the world. The system, known as Assurance Maladie, provides universal coverage to all residents, including expats who have lived in the country for at least three months. Public healthcare is funded through social security contributions and taxes, and patients are required to pay a portion of their medical expenses. However, most costs are reimbursed, and low-income individuals may be eligible for additional assistance.

Private Healthcare

In addition to the public healthcare system, France has a thriving private healthcare sector. Private hospitals and clinics offer a wide range of medical services, often with shorter waiting times and more personalized care. Some expats may choose to take out private health insurance to cover the costs of private healthcare or to supplement their public healthcare coverage.

Health Insurance

Expats living and working in France are typically required to register with the French social security system and contribute to the public healthcare system. EU citizens may also use their European Health Insurance Card (EHIC) for temporary access to healthcare while visiting France. Non-EU citizens and long-term residents should consider purchasing private health insurance to ensure full coverage and access to private healthcare facilities.

Pharmacies

Pharmacies are widely available throughout France and can be identified by a green cross sign. French pharmacies dispense prescription medications, over-the-counter drugs, and various health and wellness products. Some pharmacies offer 24-hour service, and a local on-call pharmacist can be found in case of emergencies.

Emergency Services

In case of a medical emergency, dial 15 (SAMU) for an ambulance or medical assistance, 18 for the fire department (which often provides emergency medical services), or 112 for the European emergency number. Emergency care is provided at public hospitals, and patients will be taken to the nearest appropriate facility. Emergency care is generally of high quality and widely accessible throughout France.

Specialist Care and Dentistry

France offers a wide range of specialist care, including general practitioners, paediatricians, gynaecologists, psychiatrists, and other medical professionals. Dentistry is also available, and dental care is partially covered by the public healthcare system. However, many expats opt for supplementary dental insurance to cover additional costs.

Safety and Security

While France is generally safe, it's essential for expats and visitors to remain vigilant, take standard precautions, and stay informed about local safety and security conditions. By doing so, you can enjoy your time in France with peace of mind.

General Safety

France is generally considered a safe country for residents and visitors alike. While crime rates are relatively low, it's essential to remain vigilant and take standard precautions, especially in tourist-heavy areas.

Petty Crime

As in any country, petty crimes such as pickpocketing, purse snatching, and theft can occur, particularly in crowded and touristy areas. To minimize the risk, keep your belongings secure, avoid displaying valuable items, and stay aware of your surroundings.

Terrorism

While the risk of terrorism in France has decreased in recent years, the country has experienced several high-profile attacks. The French government has implemented robust security measures, and visitors should comply with any instructions provided by local authorities. Stay informed about current events and remain vigilant in public spaces.

Scams

Scams targeting tourists can occur in France. Be cautious when approached by strangers offering unsolicited help, and avoid participating in street games or purchasing items from unlicensed vendors. If you suspect a scam, walk away and report the incident to local authorities.

Public Transport

Public transportation in France is generally safe and reliable. However, it's essential to stay vigilant and keep an eye on your belongings, especially during peak hours when pickpocketing is more likely.

Road Safety

France has well-maintained roads and highways, making driving relatively safe. However, it's essential to familiarize yourself with local driving laws, follow the speed limits, and exercise caution, especially in urban areas with heavy traffic.

Natural Disasters

France is relatively safe from severe natural disasters. However, certain regions may experience minor earthquakes, flooding, or avalanches in mountainous areas. Stay informed about local weather conditions and follow any instructions provided by local authorities.

Emergency Services

In case of an emergency, dial 17 for the police, 15 for medical assistance (SAMU), 18 for the fire department, or 112 for the European emergency number. French emergency services are generally efficient and reliable.

5. NAVIGATING SOCIAL INTERACTIONS AND ETIQUETTE

Making Friends and Building Connections

Navigating social interactions and etiquette is an important aspect of adapting to daily life in another country. Building connections and making friends with locals and other expatriates can greatly enhance your experience and help you acclimate to the culture more quickly. Here are some tips for making friends and building connections while respecting local social etiquette:

Language

Learning some basic phrases can go a long way in making friends and breaking down communication barriers. Even if your language skills are limited, locals will appreciate your effort to speak their language. Additionally, consider enrolling in a language class, which can also serve as an opportunity to meet new people and practice your language skills.

Cultural understanding

Familiarize yourself with local customs, traditions, and social norms to better understand and navigate social interactions. Being aware of and respecting local etiquette, such as greetings, table manners, and gift-giving customs, will help you make a positive impression and build rapport with locals.

Networking events and social clubs

Attend networking events, expatriate meetups, and social clubs to meet like-minded individuals and expand your social circle. There are numerous groups and organizations catering to expatriates, offering opportunities for cultural exchange, language practice, and shared interests.

Hobbies and interests

Pursue your hobbies and interests by joining clubs, teams, or classes. Participating in activities that you enjoy will provide a natural setting to connect with others who share your interests, making it easier to build friendships.

Social media and messaging apps

Social media platforms and messaging apps are usually widely used and can be an excellent tool for staying connected and organizing social events. Be sure to exchange contact information with new acquaintances and join relevant groups to stay informed about upcoming events and activities.

Be open and approachable

When interacting with locals and other expatriates, be open, approachable, and willing to engage in conversation. Share your experiences, ask questions, and show genuine interest in learning about culture and the experiences of others. Demonstrating curiosity and an open-minded attitude will make you more approachable and help you build connections more easily.

Patience and persistence

Building meaningful friendships takes time and effort, especially when navigating cultural differences. Be patient and persistent in your efforts to connect with others and remember that building strong relationships may require additional time and understanding.

Social Customs and Taboos

By familiarizing yourself with these customs and taboos, you will be better prepared to navigate social interactions and build connections in France.

Greeting Etiquette

When meeting someone for the first time, a handshake is the appropriate greeting. As you become more familiar with someone, cheek kissing (la bise) is common among friends and acquaintances. The number of kisses varies depending on the region, typically ranging from two to four.

Personal Space

The French value their personal space. When speaking with someone, maintain a comfortable distance and avoid excessive physical contact.

Addressing Others

When addressing someone you don't know well, use their title (Monsieur, Madame, or Mademoiselle) and last name. It's considered impolite to use a person's first name unless you are invited to do so.

Conversational Topics

Be cautious when discussing personal matters or controversial subjects such as religion and politics, especially with people you don't know well. Stick to neutral topics like food, art, or travel.

Dining Etiquette

At the dinner table, wait for the host to begin eating before you start. Keep your hands visible and above the table, but not your elbows. Use utensils appropriately and avoid making loud noises while eating.

Gifts

When invited to someone's home, it's customary to bring a gift such as a bottle of wine, chocolates, or flowers. Avoid giving chrysanthemums, as they are associated with funerals.

Tipping

In France, tipping is not obligatory, as a service charge is typically included in the bill. However, it is appreciated if you leave a small tip (around 5-10%) for exceptional service.

Public Behaviour

The French value politeness and decorum in public spaces. Avoid speaking loudly, chewing gum, or engaging in other potentially disruptive behaviours.

Queuing

The French tend to have a more relaxed attitude towards queuing. Be patient and respectful of others when waiting in line.

Taboos

Avoid discussing personal finances, asking about someone's salary, or inquiring about the cost of their possessions. It's also considered impolite to ask about someone's age or weight.

Dining and Food Culture

The French take great pride in their cuisine, and food plays a central role in their culture. Mealtimes are often considered an opportunity to connect with friends and family, and meals can last for several hours.

By understanding and appreciating the dining and food culture in France, you'll be better prepared to enjoy the rich culinary experiences that this country has to offer.

Variety of cuisines

Traditional Meals

A traditional French meal typically consists of several courses, beginning with an appetizer (entrée), followed by the main course (plat principal), a cheese course, and finally a dessert. Each course is usually accompanied by wine, which is considered an essential part of the dining experience.

Bread

Bread is a staple in French cuisine and is often served with every meal. It is customary to place bread directly on the table rather than on a plate. Baguettes, croissants, and pain au chocolat are popular types of bread.

Cheese

France is famous for its wide variety of cheeses. A cheese course is typically served after the main course and before dessert. It is customary to sample several different types of cheese during this course, and it is often accompanied by a glass of wine.

Wine

France is renowned for its wine production, and wine is an integral part of French dining culture. Each region of France produces its own unique variety of wines, and it is common to pair different wines with different courses during a meal.

Dining Etiquette

French dining etiquette is formal, and it is essential to be mindful of table manners. Some key points to remember include waiting for the host to begin eating before starting, keeping your hands visible above the table, using utensils properly, and refraining from making loud noises while eating.

Tipping

A service charge is usually included in the bill at restaurants, so tipping is not obligatory. However, leaving a small tip (around 5-10%) for exceptional service is appreciated.

Cafés and Pâtisseries

Cafés are a significant part of French culture, serving as social hubs where people gather to enjoy coffee, pastries, and conversation. Pâtisseries are bakeries specializing in pastries and sweets, and they are popular spots to enjoy a treat and socialize.

Regional Cuisine

French cuisine varies by region, with each area offering its unique specialties. For example, seafood dishes are prevalent in coastal regions, while hearty meat and potato dishes are more common in the mountainous areas.

Slow Food Movement

France has been a forerunner in the slow food movement, emphasizing quality ingredients, traditional preparation methods, and the enjoyment of food as a social experience. This approach to food has helped maintain a strong culinary tradition and foster a deep appreciation for the art of dining.

6. BUSINESS ETIQUETTE AND PRACTICES

Building Trust and Relationships

By understanding and adhering to these business etiquette guidelines and practices, you can build lasting relationships with your French counterparts and pave the way for a successful professional collaboration.

Importance of Relationships

In France, building strong relationships with your business partners is essential for successful collaboration. Trust, respect, and personal connections play a significant role in the decision-making process.

First Impressions

Dressing appropriately, being punctual, and addressing people formally (using "Monsieur," "Madame," or "Mademoiselle" followed by the person's last name) are crucial in making a good first impression. A firm handshake and maintaining eye contact are also important.

Business Meetings

Meetings usually start with some small talk to establish rapport and create a relaxed atmosphere. Avoid discussing personal matters or sensitive topics (such as religion, politics, or money) during these initial conversations. Be prepared for meetings to run longer than scheduled, as the French value thorough discussion and debate.

Communication Style

The French communication style is typically indirect and nuanced, with an emphasis on diplomacy and tact. Be mindful of your tone and body language, as they are considered just as important as the words you use. It's crucial to remain polite, professional, and patient when addressing any disagreements or misunderstandings.

Business Cards

Business cards should be exchanged at the beginning of a meeting. Present your card with the French side facing up (if it is bilingual) and make sure to treat the cards you receive with respect – take a moment to read them and avoid writing on them or placing them in your back pocket.

Hierarchical Structures

French businesses tend to be structured hierarchically, and decision-making authority is usually concentrated at the top levels of management. It is essential to show respect for those in positions of authority and to follow proper channels when communicating with them.

Networking

Networking is an essential aspect of building relationships in the French business world. Attend industry events, conferences, and social gatherings to expand your professional network and nurture relationships with potential business partners.

Building Trust

Be prepared to invest time in getting to know your French counterparts before discussing business matters. Sharing a meal or attending social events together can help to build trust and strengthen your relationship.

Gift-Giving

Gift-giving is not common in French business culture, but small gifts may be appropriate after a successful collaboration or to celebrate a significant milestone. If you choose to give a gift, opt for high-quality items, such as a good bottle of wine or a specialty product from your home country.

Follow-up

After meetings and events, follow up with a brief email or phone call to express your gratitude and reinforce the relationship. Maintain regular communication to keep the connection strong and demonstrate your commitment to the partnership.

Dress Code and Appearance

By adhering to these guidelines for dress code and appearance in France, you will convey a sense of respect and professionalism, while also demonstrating your understanding of French culture and social norms.

Importance of Appearance

In France, appearance is important and plays a significant role in making a good impression. Dressing appropriately for the occasion and maintaining a neat, polished appearance is essential in both professional and social settings.

Business Attire

French business attire is typically conservative and elegant. Men are expected to wear well-tailored suits in neutral colours, such as navy blue, black, or charcoal grey, with a crisp dress shirt and tie. Women should opt for a suit or dress, paired with a modest blouse, in similar colours. Accessories should be kept minimal and tasteful.

Smart Casual

For less formal events or casual office environments, smart casual attire is appropriate. This can include tailored trousers or skirts, button-down shirts or blouses, and elegant sweaters or blazers. Jeans and sneakers may be acceptable in some settings, but it's essential to ensure they are clean and well-fitting.

Social Settings

In social situations, the dress code varies depending on the type of event or venue. For upscale restaurants, theatres, or formal parties, men should wear a suit or sports jacket, while women can opt for a stylish dress or pantsuit. For more casual events or venues, neat and fashionable clothing that reflects your personal style is appropriate.

Grooming

Personal grooming is crucial in France, and both men and women should pay attention to their hair, nails, and overall hygiene. Men should be clean-shaven or maintain well-groomed facial hair, while women should keep their makeup subtle and elegant.

Accessories

When it comes to accessories, less is more in France. Both men and women should choose understated and high-quality items, such as a classic wristwatch, simple jewellery, and a stylish but functional bag or briefcase.

Perfume and Cologne

French people are known for their appreciation of fine fragrances, but it's essential to wear perfume or cologne sparingly, as strong scents can be overwhelming in professional or crowded settings.

Regional Variations

Keep in mind that dress codes and fashion preferences may vary between different regions of France. For example, Paris is known for its high fashion and sophistication, while the South of France may have a more relaxed and Mediterranean influence on style.

Business Cards and Introductions

By following these guidelines for business cards and introductions in France, you will demonstrate your understanding of French business culture and create a positive impression when networking with French professionals.

Business Card Etiquette

In France, business cards are an essential part of professional networking and are exchanged during both formal and informal meetings. Ensure your business card is clean, well-designed, and contains your name, job title, company name, contact information, and website. Having one side of the card printed in French and the other in English is a thoughtful gesture, especially if you're conducting business with French speakers.

Presenting Business Cards

When presenting your business card, use your right hand and ensure that the text is facing the recipient. Offer your card after the initial handshake and introduction, and never during a meal or social event. It is polite to present your card to everyone you meet in a professional setting, even if they are not directly involved in your business dealings.

Receiving Business Cards

When you receive a business card, take a moment to look at it carefully, and acknowledge the person's name and title. This shows respect and attentiveness. It is considered rude to write on a business card or to put it away immediately in your pocket or wallet. Instead, keep the card on the table or in a cardholder during the meeting.

Introductions

In France, introductions are an essential aspect of building professional relationships. When meeting someone for the first time, stand up, make eye contact, and offer a firm handshake. Use the person's title (Monsieur, Madame, or Mademoiselle) followed by their last name. If you have a mutual acquaintance, it is helpful to mention their name as it can help establish a connection.

Addressing People

In a professional setting, it is crucial to address people by their title and last name until they invite you to use their first name. This shows respect and formality. In more informal settings or when a relationship has become friendlier, using first names may be appropriate.

Conversational Topics

When engaging in conversation, begin with light topics such as current events, culture, or the arts before diving into business discussions. This allows both parties to establish rapport and get to know each other on a more personal level. Avoid discussing controversial topics or personal matters, as this can be seen as intrusive.

Communication Styles and Nonverbal Cues

Understanding and adapting to French communication styles and nonverbal cues will help you navigate social and professional interactions more effectively. By being attentive to these aspects of communication, you can build stronger relationships with French colleagues, friends, and acquaintances.

Communication Style

French communication tends to be formal, especially in professional settings. Politeness, diplomacy, and eloquence are highly valued. Conversations may include a mix of direct and indirect communication, with French speakers often using metaphors, analogies, and wordplay to make a point. It's important to listen carefully and ask for clarification if needed.

Nonverbal Cues

French people often use nonverbal cues and gestures to emphasize their point or express emotions. Common gestures include shrugging, raising eyebrows, and using hand movements to illustrate a point. Be aware of these gestures and try to understand the context in which they are used.

Eye Contact

Maintaining eye contact is essential in French communication, as it signifies engagement, trust, and respect. Avoiding eye contact can be interpreted as disinterest or dishonesty. However, excessive or prolonged eye contact may be considered intrusive or inappropriate, so find a balance that demonstrates attentiveness without making the other person uncomfortable.

Personal Space

The French value personal space, and it's important to maintain a respectful distance during conversations. Standing too close can be perceived as invasive, while standing too far away can be seen as disinterested or aloof. As a general guideline, maintain an arm's length distance when speaking with someone.

Touch

Physical touch is not as common in professional settings in France as it may be in other cultures. A handshake is the standard greeting, and other forms of touch, such as hugging or patting on the back, are typically reserved for closer relationships or informal situations.

Facial Expressions

French people often use facial expressions to convey their emotions or thoughts, and it is crucial to pay attention to these cues when communicating. A smile, for example, can indicate friendliness or agreement, while a frown may signify disagreement or displeasure. Be mindful of your own facial expressions to ensure that you are sending the appropriate message.

Tone of Voice

The French tend to speak in a moderate tone, and raising your voice can be considered impolite or aggressive. Keep your tone even and measured, and avoid interrupting or speaking over someone else, as this can be seen as disrespectful.

7. OFFICE CULTURE AND HIERARCHIES

Respect for Authority and Seniority

By understanding and adapting to the hierarchical nature of French office culture, you can navigate professional interactions more effectively and build successful working relationships with colleagues and superiors. Respecting authority and seniority will be essential in earning trust and respect within the organization.

Hierarchical Structure

French office culture tends to be hierarchical, with a clear distinction between different levels of management and employees. Decision-making power is often centralized at the top, and those in higher positions generally expect respect and deference from their subordinates. It's essential to understand your position within this hierarchy and interact with colleagues accordingly.

Respect for Authority

Due to the high power distance in French culture, it's crucial to show respect for authority figures, including managers and senior colleagues. This may involve using formal titles (e.g., "Monsieur," "Madame"), addressing superiors with the formal "vous" pronoun, and waiting for permission to speak in meetings. Always follow the established chain of command when communicating with others in the organization.

Seniority

In France, seniority is often valued over meritocracy, and employees with more years of experience or higher qualifications may receive preferential treatment. Be prepared to defer to senior colleagues' opinions and decisions, even if you have a different perspective. Recognize that your input may carry more weight as you gain experience and build relationships within the company.

Decision-Making Process

Due to the hierarchical nature of French office culture, decisions are typically made by those in higher positions, with limited input from subordinates. Be patient with this process, as it may be slower than in more collaborative environments. Present your ideas and suggestions to your manager, but be prepared for the possibility that they may not be implemented immediately or at all.

Formality

French office culture is generally formal, with a focus on politeness and professionalism. Be punctual for meetings and appointments, dress appropriately, and use formal language when addressing colleagues and clients. Avoid discussing personal matters at work or engaging in excessive small talk, as this may be perceived as unprofessional.

Relationship-Building

Despite the hierarchical structure, building strong relationships with colleagues is important in French office culture. Networking and participating in social events can help you establish connections that may lead to future opportunities or support within the company. Be aware that it may take time to build trust and rapport with French colleagues, so be patient and persistent in your efforts.

8. BUSINESS MEETINGS AND NEGOTIATIONS

Scheduling and Punctuality

By adhering to scheduling and punctuality norms, engaging in polite small talk, and approaching negotiations with patience and professionalism, you can navigate French business meetings more effectively and establish strong working relationships with your French colleagues.

Scheduling meetings

French business meetings are typically arranged well in advance, with invitations sent out at least a week or two before the meeting date. It is essential to confirm your attendance promptly upon receiving an invitation. Be aware that August is a common vacation period in France, so scheduling meetings during this time might be difficult, as many people will be out of the office.

Punctuality

Timekeeping is taken seriously in France, and punctuality is expected for business meetings. Arrive on time or even a few minutes early to demonstrate your professionalism and respect for your colleagues' time. If you are running late, be sure to notify the meeting organizer or your contact person as soon as possible.

Meeting Agenda

French business meetings often have a clear agenda, which is usually distributed to participants beforehand. Familiarize yourself with the agenda items and come prepared to discuss the topics at hand. Meetings may be more formal and structured than in some other cultures, with a focus on presentation and discussion of facts and figures.

Small Talk

While small talk is not as emphasized in French business culture as it is in some other countries, it is still important to engage in brief, polite conversation at the beginning of a meeting. Topics such as the weather, travel experiences, or recent news events are appropriate. Avoid discussing personal matters or controversial subjects.

Language

The official language for business meetings in France is French, although many professionals speak English as well. If you are not fluent in French, it is recommended to have an interpreter or bilingual colleague present, especially during negotiations. Learning a few basic French phrases and greetings can also make a positive impression on your French colleagues.

Negotiations

French business negotiations can be more formal and lengthy than in some other cultures. Be prepared for a detailed discussion of terms and conditions, with a focus on quality, innovation, and long-term relationships. Present your proposals with supporting data and be ready to answer questions thoroughly. Avoid high-pressure tactics or aggressive behaviour, as this may damage your credibility and harm your chances of reaching an agreement.

Meeting Structure and Protocol

By understanding and adhering to the structure and protocol of French business meetings, you can navigate these interactions more effectively and foster productive working relationships with your French colleagues.:

Meeting Organization

French business meetings tend to be more formal and structured than in some other cultures. The meeting organizer is responsible for setting the agenda, distributing it to participants in advance, and ensuring that the meeting follows the predetermined schedule.

Agenda

The agenda for French business meetings usually includes a clear outline of the topics to be discussed and the order in which they will be addressed. Stick to the agenda and be prepared to discuss each topic in depth, providing facts and figures to support your points.

Introductions

At the beginning of the meeting, the highest-ranking person in the room or the meeting organizer typically initiates introductions. Be prepared to give a brief introduction of yourself, your role, and your organization. Remember to address people using their appropriate titles (Monsieur, Madame, or Mademoiselle) followed by their last name.

Presentation Materials

Visual aids and presentation materials should be prepared in French, with any important documents translated into French as well. Ensure that your materials are clear, concise, and well-organized, as French business professionals tend to appreciate a detail-oriented approach.

Decision-Making

Decision-making in French business meetings may be slower than in some other cultures, as there is often a thorough discussion and analysis of the issues at hand. Be patient and prepared to support your proposals with evidence and reasoning. Decisions are usually made by the highest-ranking person or a small group of decision-makers, so be sure to address your points to them directly.

Meeting Etiquette

During meetings, maintain a formal and respectful tone, addressing colleagues and superiors by their titles and last names. Interruptions are generally considered impolite, so wait for an appropriate pause before speaking or asking questions. Be prepared for lively debates and discussions, as the French appreciate intellectual exchange and may challenge your ideas to stimulate conversation.

Closing the Meeting

The meeting organizer or the highest-ranking person will usually conclude the meeting by summarizing the decisions made and outlining any action items or next steps. Thank everyone for their participation and express your enthusiasm for future collaboration. Follow up with an email summarizing the key points and any agreed-upon action items.

Tips for Effective Negotiation

By implementing these tips, you can increase your chances of successful negotiations with French business professionals and foster strong, lasting partnerships:

Do your homework

Before entering into negotiations, research the French company and its representatives, as well as the market conditions and industry trends. This knowledge will help you make informed decisions and demonstrate your commitment to the partnership.

Develop relationships

Building trust and rapport with your French counterparts is crucial for successful negotiations. Invest time in getting to know them through informal interactions, such as shared meals or social events, before discussing business matters.

Be punctual

While the French may not be as strict about punctuality as some other cultures, it is still essential to arrive on time for meetings and negotiations. This shows respect for your counterparts and their time.

Maintain a professional demeanour

French business culture values formality and professionalism. Dress appropriately, address others by their titles and last names, and maintain a polite and respectful tone throughout the negotiations.

Be well-prepared

French business professionals appreciate a well-structured, detail-oriented approach. Prepare a clear proposal, supported by relevant facts and figures, and be ready to answer questions and provide additional information as needed.

Demonstrate patience

Decision-making in French negotiations may be slower than in other cultures, as there is often an emphasis on thorough analysis and discussion. Be patient and allow ample time for your counterparts to consider your proposal and consult with their colleagues.

Be willing to compromise

The French approach to negotiation often involves finding a mutually beneficial solution that meets the needs of both parties. Be open to compromise and be prepared to make concessions in order to reach an agreement.

Use clear, concise language

Avoid using jargon or overly complex language when presenting your proposal or discussing terms. The French value clarity and precision in communication.

Pay attention to nonverbal cues

Nonverbal communication can provide valuable insights into your counterparts' feelings and intentions. Be aware of body language, facial expressions, and tone of voice, and adjust your approach accordingly.

Follow up with a written agreement

Once you have reached a consensus, it is crucial to follow up with a written agreement outlining the terms and conditions. This ensures that both parties are clear on their responsibilities and helps to prevent misunderstandings down the line.

Common Mistakes to Avoid

By avoiding these common mistakes, you can foster better relationships with your French counterparts, improve the effectiveness of your meetings, and increase the likelihood of achieving your desired outcomes.

Arriving late

Punctuality is important in French business culture. Arriving late to a meeting can be perceived as disrespectful and may damage your credibility.

Informal greetings

Using informal greetings, such as addressing someone by their first name without permission, can be considered disrespectful. Always address your French counterparts with their appropriate titles and surnames until a more informal relationship is established.

Inadequate preparation

The French value thoroughness and detail-oriented presentations. Arriving at a meeting unprepared can damage your credibility and undermine the negotiation process.

Interrupting

Interrupting someone while they are speaking is considered impolite. Allow your French counterparts to finish their thoughts before responding, even if you have a pressing point to make.

Overemphasis on small talk

While relationship-building is important, French business culture values getting straight to the point in meetings. Avoid spending too much time on small talk, and instead focus on the agenda at hand.

Hard selling or aggressive tactics

The French prefer a more collaborative and diplomatic approach to negotiation. Aggressive sales tactics or pushing for an immediate decision can be off-putting and may hinder the negotiation process.

Ignoring hierarchy

French business culture is hierarchical, and it's essential to respect the chain of command. Addressing someone lower in the hierarchy before consulting their superior can be perceived as disrespectful.

Overuse of humour

While humour can help break the ice in some situations, it's essential to maintain a professional demeanour in business meetings. Avoid using humour excessively or making jokes that could be considered inappropriate.

Excessive use of gestures and body language

The French tend to be more reserved in their nonverbal communication. Avoid using exaggerated gestures, as they may be perceived as unprofessional or even rude.

Neglecting follow-up

Following up on agreed-upon actions and commitments is crucial for maintaining trust and credibility. Ensure that you follow up promptly after the meeting and provide updates on progress as necessary.

9. BUSINESS DINING AND ENTERTAINMENT

Traditional Hospitality

Traditional French hospitality is characterized by warm greetings, polite interactions, and an emphasis on sharing food and conversation. By understanding and adhering to these customs, you can fully enjoy the rich experiences that French hospitality has to offer.

Warm greetings

A firm handshake is the common greeting in France, while close friends and family members may exchange kisses on the cheeks (known as "la bise"). It is essential to greet everyone present when entering or leaving a social gathering.

Politeness and formality

French people often address each other using formal titles (such as "Monsieur" or "Madame") and last names until a closer relationship is established. Good manners and etiquette are highly valued.

Invitations

When invited to a French home, it is customary to bring a small gift, such as flowers, chocolates, or a bottle of wine. Arrive on time or slightly late, as punctuality is appreciated, but not to the extent that it would be in some other cultures.

Dining

French cuisine is renowned worldwide, and sharing a meal is an essential aspect of French hospitality. Hosts will typically serve multiple courses, often including an appetizer, main course, cheese course, and dessert. Be prepared for lively conversation and leisurely dining, as meals can last several hours.

Table manners

Proper table etiquette is crucial when dining with French hosts. Wait for the host to begin eating before starting, keep your hands visible on the table (but not your elbows), and do not begin drinking until a toast has been made.

Appreciation

Show your appreciation for your host's efforts by complimenting the food, the home, or their hospitality. It is also polite to send a thank-you note or make a phone call after the event to express your gratitude.

Reciprocity

If you have been a guest in a French home, it is customary to reciprocate by inviting your hosts to your home or organizing a gathering in their honour.

10. LEISURE, ENTERTAINMENT AND FAMILY ACTIVITIES

Exploring Natural Wonders

France boasts a diverse range of natural wonders, from stunning coastlines and picturesque countryside to majestic mountain ranges and breathtaking national parks. Here are some of the top natural attractions in France:

Mont Blanc

Located in the French Alps, **Mont Blanc** is the highest mountain in Western Europe, standing at 15,774 feet (4,808 meters). Chamonix, a popular base for mountaineering, skiing, and hiking, offers stunning views of Mont Blanc and the surrounding peaks.

Gorges du Verdon

Often called the "Grand Canyon of Europe," the **Gorges du Verdon** is a spectacular river canyon in the Provence-Alpes-Côte d'Azur region. With its turquoise waters and dramatic limestone cliffs, it offers opportunities for hiking, rock climbing, and water sports.

Calanques de Cassis

Located along the Mediterranean coast between Marseille and Cassis, the **Calanques** are a series of rocky inlets featuring turquoise waters and dramatic limestone cliffs. Visitors can hike, swim, or take a boat tour to explore this stunning coastal landscape.

Camargue

A vast wetland in the South of France, the **Camargue** is home to unique flora and fauna, including wild horses, pink flamingos, and bulls. The area offers birdwatching, horseback riding, and opportunities to explore traditional French ranches called "manades."

The Dune of Pilat

Situated on the Atlantic coast in the Arcachon Bay area, the **Dune of Pilat** is the tallest sand dune in Europe, reaching a height of 110 meters (360 feet). Visitors can climb the dune for panoramic views of the surrounding landscape, including the Atlantic Ocean, pine forests, and the bay.

Étretat Cliffs

These striking **white chalk cliffs** and natural arches along the Normandy coast have inspired many artists, including Claude Monet. Hiking trails offer breathtaking views of the cliffs and the English Channel.

Jardin des Plantes

Located in Paris, the **Jardin des Plantes** is a historic botanical garden that provides a serene escape from the bustling city. With numerous themed gardens, greenhouses, and a small zoo, the garden is a perfect destination for nature lovers.

The Pyrenees

A mountain range forming the natural border between France and Spain, the **Pyrenees** offers a variety of outdoor activities, including skiing, hiking, and cycling. The region is also home to several national parks, such as the **Pyrénées National Park** and the **Aigüestortes i Estany de Sant Maurici National Park**.

Historic Sites and Cultural Attractions

France is home to numerous historic sites and cultural attractions that showcase its rich history and heritage. Here are some of the most famous and significant sites to visit:

Eiffel Tower

An iconic symbol of Paris and France, the **Eiffel Tower** was built for the 1889 World's Fair. Visitors can climb or take an elevator to the top for panoramic views of the city.

Louvre Museum

One of the world's largest and most visited art museums, the **Louvre** houses a vast collection of art, including the famous Mona Lisa and the Venus de Milo.

Palace of Versailles

A symbol of royal extravagance, the **Palace of Versailles** was the residence of the French monarchy from 1682 until the French Revolution. The palace's lavish interiors, extensive gardens, and the Hall of Mirrors are must-see attractions.

Notre-Dame Cathedral

A masterpiece of Gothic architecture, the **Notre-Dame Cathedral** in Paris is known for its stunning stained glass windows, flying buttresses, and the iconic gargoyles that adorn its façade.

Mont-Saint-Michel

This medieval monastery and village are perched on a rocky island off the coast of Normandy. With its dramatic setting and well-preserved architecture, <u>Mont-Saint-Michel</u> is a UNESCO World Heritage site.

Château de Chambord

One of the most famous châteaux in the Loire Valley, <u>Chambord</u> is an impressive example of French Renaissance architecture. Its distinctive double-helix staircase and intricate roofscape make it a popular tourist attraction.

Roman ruins in Arles and Nîmes

The cities of Arles and <u>Nîmes</u> are home to some of the best-preserved Roman ruins in France, including the <u>Arles Amphitheatre</u>, the <u>Maison Carrée</u> in Nîmes, and the <u>Pont du Gard</u> aqueduct.

Carcassonne

A UNESCO World Heritage site, the fortified city of <u>Carcassonne</u> in southern France is known for its medieval walls, towers, and narrow, cobblestone streets.

Lascaux Cave

Located in south-western France, the <u>Lascaux Cave</u> contains some of the most famous prehistoric cave paintings, dating back around 15,000 years.

The Catacombs of Paris

An underground ossuary holding the remains of millions of Parisians, the <u>Catacombs</u> offer a unique and eerie glimpse into the city's past.

Musée d'Orsay

Housed in a former railway station, the <u>Musée d'Orsay</u> in Paris is home to an extensive collection of Impressionist and Post-Impressionist art, including works by Monet, Renoir, and Van Gogh.

Sainte-Chappelle

Located on the Île de la Cité in Paris, the <u>Sainte-Chapelle</u> is a stunning example of Gothic architecture, known for its remarkable stained glass windows that depict over 1,000 biblical scenes.

Family-Friendly Activities and Entertainment

France offers numerous family-friendly activities and entertainment options that cater to visitors of all ages. Here are some popular attractions and activities to consider:

Disneyland Paris

This **world-renowned theme park** is the perfect destination for families, with exciting rides, shows, and attractions based on Disney characters and stories.

Parc Astérix

Based on the famous French comic book series, this **amusement park** near Paris features roller coasters, water rides, and shows inspired by the adventures of Astérix and Obélix.

La Villette Science Museum (Cité des Sciences et de l'Industrie)

Located in Paris, this **interactive science museum** offers hands-on exhibits, workshops, and demonstrations for children and adults alike.

Océanopolis

Situated in **Brest**, this marine centre features a variety of aquariums and exhibits showcasing marine life from around the world, including polar, tropical, and temperate zones.

Puy du Fou

An award-winning historical theme park in western France, **Puy du Fou** offers spectacular live shows and immersive experiences that transport visitors through different periods of French history.

Futuroscope

Located near Poitiers, this **futuristic theme park** offers unique attractions and shows focused on multimedia, cinema, and cutting-edge technology.

Zoological Parks

France is home to several excellent zoos, such as the **ZooParc de Beauval**, **La Palmyre Zoo**, and the **Zoological Park of Paris**, where families can observe and learn about a wide range of animal species.

Gouffre de Padirac

This massive **underground cave system** in the Midi-Pyrénées region offers guided tours by boat and on foot, providing a fascinating adventure for families.

The Little Prince Park (Parc du Petit Prince)

Inspired by the beloved French novella, this **theme park** in eastern France features attractions, shows, and activities related to the world of the Little Prince.

Beaches and coastal activities

France boasts numerous beautiful beaches along its coastline, offering opportunities for swimming, sunbathing, water sports, and seaside exploration.

Outdoor activities

Enjoy family-friendly outdoor activities such as hiking, biking, and horseback riding in France's diverse landscapes, including the French Alps, the Pyrenees, and the lush countryside.

Interactive museums and cultural sites

Many French museums and cultural sites, such as the Louvre and Château de Versailles, offer family-oriented tours and workshops to engage children in learning about art, history, and culture.

Celebrations and Festivals

France has a vibrant calendar of celebrations and festivals throughout the year. Some of the most popular and well-known events include:

Bastille Day (La Fête Nationale)

Held on July 14th, this **national holiday** commemorates the storming of the Bastille in 1789 and the birth of the French Republic. The day is marked by parades, fireworks, and various festivities across the country, with the largest military parade taking place on the Champs-Élysées in Paris.

Cannes Film Festival

An annual prestigious **film festival** held in Cannes, showcasing new films and documentaries from around the world. The event, usually held in May, attracts international celebrities and film industry professionals.

Nice Carnival

One of the largest **carnivals** in the world, this two-week-long event takes place in February in the city of Nice. The festival features colourful parades, floats, and street performances, culminating in the burning of the King of Carnival.

Fête de la Musique

Held annually on June 21st, this nationwide **music festival** celebrates the summer solstice with free concerts and street performances in cities and towns across France.

Interceltique Festival

This annual event in **Lorient, Brittany**, celebrates Celtic culture with music, dance, and art from various Celtic nations. The festival takes place in August and attracts thousands of visitors from around the world.

Christmas Markets

From late November to December, towns and cities across France host traditional Christmas markets, where visitors can purchase festive food, gifts, and decorations while enjoying the holiday atmosphere.

La Fête des Lumières

Held annually in December, this unique **festival of lights in Lyon** transforms the city with stunning light installations, projections, and performances.

Paris Fashion Week

This **prestigious event**, held twice a year, showcases the latest collections from top fashion designers and attracts celebrities and fashion enthusiasts from around the world.

Tour de France

This **world-famous annual cycling** race covers various routes throughout France, taking place over three weeks in July. Spectators line the streets to cheer on the cyclists and enjoy the festive atmosphere.

Festival d'Avignon

One of the oldest and **most prestigious performing arts festivals** in the world, the Festival d'Avignon takes place in July and features theatre, dance, and music performances in various venues throughout the city.

11. PRACTICAL TIPS FOR TRAVELLERS AND EXPATS

Safety and Security Tips

By following these safety and security tips, you can minimize risks and ensure a more enjoyable stay in France.

Be aware of your surroundings

Stay vigilant in crowded tourist areas, public transportation, and around major attractions, as pickpocketing and petty theft can occur. Keep your personal belongings secure and avoid displaying valuables or large sums of cash.

Emergency numbers

Familiarize yourself with the local emergency numbers. In France, dial 112 for general emergencies, 17 for police, 15 for medical emergencies, and 18 for fire services.

Research neighbourhoods

Before choosing accommodation, research neighbourhoods to find the safest and most suitable areas for your needs. Some areas may have higher crime rates or be less tourist-friendly than others.

Travel insurance

Ensure you have appropriate travel insurance covering medical expenses, theft, and other potential issues. Keep a copy of your insurance details and emergency contact information with you at all times.

Be cautious at night

Stick to well-lit and populated areas when walking at night. Avoid shortcuts through unlit or unfamiliar areas, and be cautious when using ATMs in isolated locations.

Road safety

Familiarize yourself with local traffic rules and regulations. Be cautious when crossing the street, as drivers may not always yield to pedestrians. When driving, stay within speed limits and avoid using your phone or engaging in other distractions.

Public transportation

Use reputable transportation services and avoid unlicensed taxis. Be aware of your belongings on public transportation, as theft can occur in crowded situations.

Be cautious with alcohol

Drink responsibly and avoid excessive alcohol consumption, which can impair your judgment and make you more vulnerable to crime.

Stay connected

Keep a charged mobile phone with you and ensure you have a reliable means of communication in case of emergencies.

Be respectful of local customs and laws

Familiarize yourself with local laws, customs, and etiquette to avoid inadvertently offending residents or getting into legal trouble.

Register with your embassy

If you're staying in France for an extended period, register with your country's embassy or consulate. This will facilitate communication and assistance in case of an emergency.

Stay informed

Keep up-to-date with local news and any potential safety concerns or warnings for travellers. Adjust your plans and activities accordingly if necessary.

Healthcare and insurance

Healthcare in France is known for its high quality and accessibility. The French healthcare system, called Sécurité Sociale, is a mix of public and private providers and is one of the best in the world. Both residents and expats can access healthcare services, but it's essential to have adequate health insurance to cover costs.

Public healthcare system

The French public healthcare system is funded by the government, employers, and employee contributions. Most French residents are covered by the public system, which reimburses a significant portion of medical costs, such as doctor visits, hospital stays, and prescription medications.

Private healthcare

Private healthcare in France exists alongside the public system. Many residents and expats choose to purchase supplementary private health insurance (mutuelle) to cover expenses not fully reimbursed by the public system, such as dental care, eye care, and alternative therapies.

European Health Insurance Card (EHIC)

European Union (EU) citizens can use the EHIC to access public healthcare services in France at reduced costs or sometimes for free. However, the EHIC doesn't cover all medical expenses, so it's essential to have additional travel insurance or private health insurance.

Health insurance for non-EU citizens

Non-EU citizens must have private health insurance to cover medical costs while in France. Before traveling, ensure your insurance policy covers medical treatment, hospitalization, and repatriation in case of emergency. If you plan to work or live in France, you may be eligible to enrol in the French public healthcare system and should consider purchasing supplementary private insurance.

Finding a doctor or specialist

In France, you can choose your doctor (general practitioner) and any specialist you wish to see. Some doctors and specialists work in both public and private sectors, while others only practice in one. Check if your insurance covers visits to your chosen healthcare provider.

Pharmacies

Pharmacies in France are easy to find and can provide over-the-counter medications and advice for minor health issues. Prescription medications can only be obtained with a valid prescription from a French doctor.

Emergencies

In case of emergency, call 112 for general emergencies, 15 for medical emergencies, or go to the nearest emergency room (urgences). Make sure to have your identification, insurance details, and a list of any current medications with you.

12. OVERCOMING STEREOTYPES AND PREJUDICES

Common Misconceptions and Stereotypes

It is important to recognize that stereotypes and misconceptions are oversimplified representations of a culture and should not be taken as accurate portrayals of an entire population. When engaging with French people and experiencing the culture firsthand, keep an open mind and avoid relying on stereotypes to form your opinions. There are numerous misconceptions and stereotypes about France and its people, which can sometimes lead to misunderstandings. Some common stereotypes include:

French people are rude

While it's true that the French may appear more reserved or less effusive than people from other cultures, this is often a matter of different communication styles. The French generally value politeness, discretion, and formality in social interactions. Understanding these cultural differences can help avoid taking perceived aloofness or curtness personally.

Everyone in France speaks English

While many French people, especially in urban areas, speak English to some degree, it's important not to assume that everyone is fluent or comfortable speaking in English. Making an effort to learn some basic French phrases can go a long way in facilitating communication and demonstrating respect for the local culture.

French people only eat baguettes, cheese, and drink wine

While these items are undoubtedly popular in France, the country boasts a diverse culinary landscape with regional specialties and an array of dishes that go beyond the clichés. French cuisine is known for its quality, variety, and emphasis on fresh, local ingredients.

French people are always on strike

Strikes do happen in France, and the French are known for their willingness to protest and stand up for their rights. However, the image of a perpetually striking nation is an exaggeration. Strikes occur in various sectors and are often short-lived, with life resuming as usual once the issues have been resolved.

French people are all fashionable

The stereotype of the impeccably dressed Parisian is not representative of the entire population. While France is famous for its fashion industry, and some people take great pride in their appearance, clothing styles vary widely, and not everyone follows the latest trends.

All French people are romantic and great lovers

While France, particularly Paris, is often associated with romance, it is unfair and unrealistic to generalize this stereotype to the entire population. Relationships and attitudes towards love and romance vary among individuals, just as they do in any other country.

France is synonymous with Paris

Paris is undoubtedly the most famous city in France, but the country has much more to offer. Each region has its unique culture, history, cuisine, and landscape, which are often quite different from those of the capital. To truly experience France, it's essential to explore beyond Paris and discover the diverse beauty of the country.

Strategies for overcoming biases and promoting understanding

As with any foreign country, it's important to approach a new culture with an open mind and a willingness to learn about its culture and people. Here are some strategies for overcoming biases and promoting understanding:

Learn about the culture and history

Learn about the culture and history before visiting or living in the country. This can help you gain a better understanding of the customs, traditions, and beliefs of its people.

Engage with the local community

Engage with the local community to learn about their daily lives, customs, and traditions. This can help you develop a deeper appreciation and understanding of their culture.

Avoid stereotypes and assumptions

Avoid making assumptions or generalizations about the people or culture. Recognize that diversity exists within the country and that each individual has their own unique experiences and perspectives.

Be respectful and open-minded

Be respectful and open-minded when interacting with locals. Show interest in their culture and traditions and avoid imposing your own beliefs or values.

Learn the language

Learn some basic phrases to help you communicate with the local community. This can help you build rapport and establish a deeper connection with the people.

Participate in cultural activities

Participate in cultural activities such as festivals and ceremonies to learn more about the customs and traditions of the local community. This can also help you build relationships and connect with others.

Seek out diverse perspectives

Seek out diverse perspectives on the country and its culture, including those of different ethnic groups and social classes. This can help you gain a more nuanced and comprehensive understanding of the country and its people.

13. BUILDING CROSS-CULTURAL RELATIONSHIPS

Effective Communication and Conflict Resolution

Effective communication and conflict resolution are key components of building cross-cultural relationships. Here are some tips for expats on effective communication and conflict resolution:

Learn the language

Learning some basic phrases can help you communicate more effectively with the local community. This can help you establish rapport and build relationships with locals.

Be aware of nonverbal cues

Be aware of nonverbal cues such as body language and tone of voice, which can vary depending on the culture. People may use indirect communication and nonverbal cues to express their thoughts and feelings, so it's important to be sensitive to these cues.

Listen actively

Active listening is an important part of effective communication. Take the time to listen to the perspectives and concerns of locals and show that you understand and value their opinions.

Be respectful

Be respectful of the culture and traditions. Show interest and respect for their beliefs and customs and avoid imposing your own values or beliefs.

Avoid confrontation

Nationals may avoid confrontation or direct conflict, preferring instead to use indirect communication and negotiation. Be mindful of this and avoid being confrontational in your communication style.

Seek to understand

Seek to understand the perspective and context in any conflict or disagreement. This can help you find common ground and work towards a mutually acceptable solution.

Be patient

Building cross-cultural relationships takes time and patience. Be patient in your communication and conflict resolution and be willing to compromise and find creative solutions.

Adapting to cultural differences

Adapting to cultural differences is an important part of living as an expat. Here are some tips for expats on how to adapt to cultural differences:

Learn about the culture

Learn about the culture and customs before you arrive. This can help you understand the social norms, values, and beliefs.

Respect local customs

Respect local customs and traditions, even if they are different from what you are used to. Show interest in the culture and be willing to learn and adapt.

Develop relationships

Develop relationships with locals, whether it's with colleagues, neighbours, or friends. This can help you gain a better understanding of the culture and develop a support network.

Learn the language

Learning some basic phrases can help you communicate more effectively with locals and show that you respect their culture.

Be patient

Be patient and understanding of cultural differences. Locals may have a different sense of time, communication style, and decision-making process than what you are used to.

Be flexible

Be flexible and adaptable in your approach to work and socializing. Locals may have different work and social customs, so be willing to adjust your expectations and approach.

Embrace new experiences

Embrace new experiences and try new things, such as trying local food, attending cultural events, or visiting new places. This can help you appreciate and enjoy the unique aspects of the culture.

Developing empathy and cultural intelligence

Developing empathy and cultural intelligence is essential for fostering meaningful cross-cultural relationships, both personally and professionally. In this chapter, we will discuss strategies and tips for cultivating empathy and cultural intelligence to better connect with people from different backgrounds.

Educate yourself about different cultures.

Invest time in learning about the values, customs, and traditions of various cultures, especially those you frequently interact with. Understanding cultural nuances can help you appreciate their perspectives and anticipate potential communication challenges.

Engage in active listening.

Make a conscious effort to listen attentively to others, without interrupting or imposing your own opinions. Active listening can help you gain deeper insights into their experiences, feelings, and perspectives, which is crucial for developing empathy.

Practice perspective-taking.

Put yourself in the shoes of others and try to understand their thoughts, emotions, and experiences from their point of view. This can help you appreciate the challenges they face and foster empathy and understanding.

Develop emotional intelligence.

Emotional intelligence refers to the ability to recognize, understand, and manage your own emotions and the emotions of others. Enhancing your emotional intelligence can help you better understand the emotional underpinnings of cross-cultural interactions and respond more empathetically.

Be curious and open-minded.

Approach cultural differences with curiosity and an open mind. Ask questions and seek to learn more about the experiences and perspectives of others, without judgment or preconceived notions.

Observe and reflect on cultural interactions.

Pay close attention to how you and others respond to cultural differences in various contexts. Reflect on these interactions to identify areas where you can improve your empathy and cultural intelligence.

Seek diverse experiences and relationships.

Expose yourself to diverse experiences and relationships by interacting with people from different cultural backgrounds. These experiences can help you develop a broader understanding of the world and enhance your empathy and cultural intelligence.

Foster a growth mindset.

Embrace a growth mindset, which involves viewing challenges as opportunities for learning and growth. This mindset can help you approach cultural differences with a willingness to learn and adapt, rather than feeling threatened or overwhelmed.

Participate in cultural training and workshops.

Consider attending workshops or participating in cultural training programs to enhance your understanding of different cultures and develop your empathy and cultural intelligence.

Continuously learn and adapt.

Recognize that developing empathy and cultural intelligence is an ongoing process that requires continuous learning, reflection, and adaptation. Stay committed to personal growth and be open to feedback and new experiences.

14. CASE STUDIES AND REAL LIFE EXAMPLES

Stories and anecdotes illustrating cultural challenges and successes

Adapting to the French approach to time and punctuality

An American expat working in France was initially frustrated by the seemingly relaxed approach to punctuality in social situations. They were used to arriving promptly for social events in the U.S., and when they did the same in France, they often found themselves waiting for a long time before other guests showed up. Over time, they learned to adapt to the more flexible approach to time in French culture and became more comfortable with the idea of arriving fashionably late.

Learning to navigate the French workplace hierarchy

A British professional working in a French company struggled initially with the more formal and hierarchical structure in their workplace. They were used to a more egalitarian environment in the UK and found it challenging to adapt to the expectations for showing deference to superiors in the French workplace. Through conversations with colleagues and observing others, they gradually learned to strike the right balance between maintaining their own perspective while also respecting the authority of their superiors.

The importance of language and communication

An Australian expat living in France realized the importance of learning the local language to connect with the French people better. Despite being able to speak English with some of their French friends, they found that making an effort to learn French went a long way in fostering deeper connections and understanding the nuances of French culture. Over time, their language skills improved, and they felt more integrated into their community.

Embracing the French dining culture

A Canadian family living in France found it challenging to adapt to the slower-paced dining culture. They were accustomed to quick meals and found that the French placed a much greater emphasis on savouring food and conversation during meals. As they began to appreciate the value of taking time to enjoy their meals, they discovered that they were building stronger relationships with their French friends, and their overall quality of life improved.

Navigating French bureaucracy

An Indian entrepreneur starting a business in France faced the challenge of navigating the often-complex French bureaucracy. They initially found the process overwhelming and struggled to understand the various regulations and requirements. By seeking advice from local experts and learning to be patient and persistent, they were able to successfully navigate the system and establish their business in France.

Lessons learned and best practices

The case studies and examples illustrate the importance of cultural awareness and adaptation when visiting or living in a foreign culture. Here are some lessons learned and best practices for navigating cultural challenges and embracing local customs:

Learn about the culture and customs

Before traveling to or living in there, take the time to research and understand the country's history, culture, traditions, and customs. This knowledge will help you avoid misunderstandings, build relationships, and appreciate the richness of the culture.

Be open-minded and adaptable

Recognize that cultural norms and practices may differ from what you're used to. Be willing to adapt your behaviour and communication style to show respect and appreciation for the local culture.

Practice patience and humility

When faced with cultural differences or challenges, remain patient and humble. Be willing to learn from others and ask for help or guidance when needed.

Develop language skills

Even basic knowledge of the language can help you connect with locals, navigate daily life, and show respect for the culture. Practice speaking, listening, and reading to enhance your communication skills and overall experience.

Observe and learn from locals

Pay attention to how locals interact, communicate, and behave in various situations. Learning from observation can provide valuable insights into cultural norms and expectations.

Show respect for religious customs and traditions

Be aware of local customs and etiquette when visiting religious sites, such as temples. Dress modestly, remove your shoes, and follow any specific guidelines provided.

Be aware of nonverbal communication

Most cultures place great importance on nonverbal cues, such as facial expressions, body language, and tone of voice. Be attentive to these cues and learn to interpret them accurately to avoid misunderstandings.

Choose ethical and responsible tourism options

Support local communities and protect the environment by choosing sustainable and responsible travel experiences. Be mindful of your impact on the local culture, environment, and economy.

Build relationships

Invest time and effort in building relationships with people, whether they are colleagues, neighbours, or friends. Developing strong connections can lead to a deeper understanding of the culture and a more fulfilling experience.

Reflect on your experiences

Take the time to reflect on your experiences, challenges, and successes. Consider what you have learned and how you can continue to grow and adapt to different cultural contexts.

Resources and Further Reading

Books, articles, and websites for further exploration

Books:

- " "Sixty Million Frenchmen Can't Be Wrong: Why We Love France but Not the French" by Jean-Benoît Nadeau and Julie Barlow - A well-researched and insightful book that delves into the complexities of French culture, society, and history.
- "A Year in Provence" by Peter Mayle - A humorous and entertaining account of an Englishman's experiences living in the French countryside.
- "The Bonjour Effect: The Secret Codes of French Conversation Revealed" by Julie Barlow and Jean-Benoît Nadeau - A guide to understanding and navigating French social customs and communication styles.
- "The Culture Map: Breaking Through the Invisible Boundaries of Global Business" by Erin Meyer - A book exploring the differences in communication, leadership, and decision-making styles across various cultures, including France.

Articles:

- "Understanding French Culture: What You Need to Know" - Expatica: https://www.expatica.com/fr/moving/integration/understanding-french-culture-104694/
- "Working in France: The Office Culture and Hierarchy" - The Local: https://www.thelocal.fr/20180413/working-in-france-the-office-culture-and-hierarchy/

Websites:

- France Diplomatie - Cultural Resources: https://www.diplomatie.gouv.fr/en/country-files/france/france-facts/cultural-resources/
- Institut Français: https://www.institutfrancais.com/en - Promotes French culture, language, and art around the world and offers resources for learning about France.
- Alliance Française: http://www.alliancefr.org/en - A global network of organizations promoting French language and culture, offering classes and cultural events.
- Expatica France: https://www.expatica.com/fr/ - A comprehensive resource for expats living in France, covering topics such as culture, lifestyle, healthcare, and education.
- The Local France: https://www.thelocal.fr/ - An English-language news site covering French news, culture, and events.

Language learning resources and cultural organisations

Language Learning Resources:

- Duolingo (https://www.duolingo.com/) - A popular language learning app that offers gamified lessons in French for learners at different levels.

- Babbel (https://www.babbel.com/) - A language learning platform with interactive lessons and real-life dialogue scenarios to help you learn French.

- Memrise (https://www.memrise.com/) - Offers courses in French vocabulary and grammar using spaced repetition and mnemonic techniques to make learning more engaging and effective.

- FluentU (https://www.fluentu.com/) - A language learning platform that uses authentic French videos, such as movie trailers, music videos, and news clips, with interactive subtitles and quizzes to help you improve your listening comprehension and vocabulary.

- Coffee Break French (https://radiolingua.com/coffeebreakfrench/) - A podcast series that teaches French through short, engaging lessons that fit into your daily routine.

Cultural Organizations:

- Alliance Française (http://www.alliancefr.org/en) - A global network of organizations promoting French language and culture, offering classes, cultural events, and resources for learning about France.

- Institut Français (https://www.institutfrancais.com/en) - Promotes French culture, language, and art around the world, and offers resources for learning about France.

- La Maison Française (https://lamaisonfrancaise.org/) - A cultural center located in various cities around the world, offering French language classes, cultural events, and opportunities to engage with the French-speaking community.

- France-Amériques (https://www.france-ameriques.org/) - A non-profit organization that fosters cultural and educational exchanges between France and the Americas, organizing events, conferences, and exhibitions related to French culture and history.

- French-American Chamber of Commerce (https://www.faccnyc.org/) - A network of organizations that supports trade and investment between France and the United States, offering networking events, seminars, and resources for learning about French business culture.

We know you appreciate how valuable reviews are to both the creators and the potential buyers of a book. Reviews help authors to improve their writing and encourage them to continue creating content that readers enjoy. They also help other readers to make informed decisions about whether a book is right for them.

So, if you have purchased this book and found it helpful, informative, or enjoyable, we implore you to take a few minutes to leave a review. Your feedback could be the deciding factor for someone else trying to decide whether to buy this book or not.

Your review doesn't need to be lengthy or formal, just an honest account of your experience with the book. Even a few sentences can make a big difference or just a simple rating. So please, consider leaving a review and help support the author and potential readers in making an informed decision.

We would love to hear from you on what you found works / doesn't work / needs more information / needs an amendment or even a new addition (for which we will credit you).

contact@wallaceline.com.au

www.ingramcontent.com/pod-product-compliance
Lightning Source LLC
Chambersburg PA
CBHW070449220526
45466CB00004B/1789